THE CRISIS WITHIN

Books by G. N. Devy

Critical Thought
After Amnesia
In Another Tongue
Of Many Heroes: An Indian Essay in Literary Historiography Indian Literary Criticism: Theory and Interpretation
A Nomad Called Thief: Reflections in Adivasi Silence
The G. N. Devy Reader

Edited by G. N. Devy
India Between Tradition and Modernity (co-editor)
Painted Words: An Anthology of Tribal Literature (editor)

THE CRISIS WITHIN

ON KNOWLEDGE AND EDUCATION IN INDIA

G. N. DEVY

ALEPH

ALEPH BOOK COMPANY
An independent publishing firm
promoted by *Rupa Publications India*

First published in India in 2017
by Aleph Book Company
7/16 Ansari Road, Daryaganj
New Delhi 110 002

Copyright © G. N. Devy 2017

All rights reserved.

The author has asserted his moral rights.

The views and opinions expressed in this book are the
author's own and the facts are as reported by him, which
have been verified to the extent possible, and the publishers
are not in any way liable for the same.

No part of this publication may be reproduced, transmitted,
or stored in a retrieval system, in any form or by any means,
without permission in writing from Aleph Book Company.

ISBN: 978-93-83064-10-6

1 3 5 7 9 10 8 6 4 2

Printed and bound in India by

This book is sold subject to the condition that it shall not,
by way of trade or otherwise, be lent, resold, hired out, or
otherwise circulated without the publisher's prior consent in
any form of binding or cover other than that in which it is
published.

For Rashmi,
the light of my family

CONTENTS

~

Introduction ix

ONE

The Crisis of Knowledge 1

TWO

Memory and Knowledge 27

THREE

Memory of the Forgotten 50

FOUR

Post-memory Education 76

Acknowledgements 109
Notes and References 111
Bibliography 119
Index 125

INTRODUCTION

The present century is often described as the 'knowledge century'. We cannot be sure if this tag will stay valid until the end of the century or whether future historians will characterize this period as the 'Age of Knowledge' as has been the case with the Dark Ages or the Age of Reason in the past. Perhaps the description sums up the euphoria resulting from the information explosion and the technologies surrounding the exponential growth in the information generated every passing second. It is possible that this epithet may not be sufficiently adequate for characterizing our time. The century has also been forecast to be the era of water wars, an age of deathless humans, an epoch of ecological termination, and the moment for an irreversible merger of the physical and the digital. The 'knowledge century' label is open to discussion and is not incontestable. Indeed, self perceptions of human civilizations can change quite radically over a relatively short temporal span. But if at all the present century can be viewed as a unique era in human history, marking a new kind of engagement with what is considered 'knowledge', it would be interesting to reflect on where India stands in relation to this new turn in history.

Numerically speaking, in 2017, nearly one in every six human beings is an Indian. This number, a staggering 1.34 billion (134 crores) out of an estimated world total of 7.4 billion (748 crores), is unprecedented in scale, and is next only to the Chinese population—1.38 billion (138 crores). In 2011, the year in which the last census was carried out, India's population stood at 1.21 billion, while the Chinese population counted a year earlier was 1.31 billion. In a few years, India will surpass China's population level. Also, the demographic proportion of the younger population in India at present is the largest ever in India's history, with more than half of the population below the age of twenty-five. Of the entire global population, nearly one in every twelve humans is a young Indian for whom meaningful education is the most assured means of finding a decent livelihood.

Education, knowledge production and research leading to widening of the horizons of thought and imagination, therefore, ought to be seen as important concerns of our time. The figures mentioned here provide only a very broad quantitative measure of the challenge before us. Considerations of how and how much knowledge is produced, how it is transacted and how it is responding to social inequalities and ecological disconnect add to the vastness and complexities involved in a study of knowledge and education in India. This book about the status of education in India, particularly higher education and the forms of knowledge that it pursues, is a modest attempt at unravelling some of the complexities. It is not intended to be a comprehensive report on education in India, nor does it hope to provide an exhaustive analysis of our knowledge status. Though knowledge and education are its twin central themes, I must at once clarify that this is not an academic book. Having spent close to half a century in and around universities, and having elsewhere presented academic research and essays, I thought it not too inappropriate to present my observations on the theme through a reflective statement. I do not intend to present a position or positions in it. Quite often, analytical studies have a purely subjective weave as their flip side, a tacit class bias presented as 'objective' culture-critique. To the extent possible, I have avoided such analysis. I would therefore like to describe this book as the 'reflections' of a person for whom knowledge and education have been serious concerns for several decades.

When I began working as a young researcher in literary studies in the early post-Independence years, the colonial experience was the obsessive interest of the day. Most forms of formal knowledge, scientific disciplines and social sciences were seen as having originated in the colonial 'transfer of knowledge'. Scholarly debates revolved around the question of acceptance or rejection of these forms of knowledge. These debates were happening in several disciplines, if not all of them, ranging from history to literature, architecture to aesthetics; but invariably the reference point was the knowledge of the colonial mint.

During the 1980s, the interest started shifting to discussion of disparities inherent in every intellectual transaction between the colonizing Western cultures and the post-colonial societies. These discussions were fascinating and produced several works of great brilliance. They gained in significance as similar discussions had been taking place in other post-colonial cultures. In Western intellectual circles too colonialism and post-colonialism acquired as much centrality as the Cold War and imperialism had enjoyed earlier. I have chosen to overlook in this book many of the valuable insights generated over the decades in both these phases as they are by now well-settled in the arena of the history of cultural relations. Given, however, the significance of the enormous amount of descriptive and analytical studies that those two moves produced, both within India and outside, I begin by briefly alluding to some of the iconic period-statements in the next section, before moving to the discussion of the more contemporary, and no less significant phenomena having a profound bearing on the question of 'knowledge' and education in India. These phenomena include the rapidly sinking fortunes of 'natural memory', technology of knowledge incubation and knowledge reception, and the sanitization of 'knowledge' effected through several exclusions—linguistic, ethnic and epistemic. This book, therefore, reflects on the condition and crisis of knowledge as much as it is, by implication, about the condition and crisis of our democracy. In order to analyse the present status of 'knowledge' in India and the problems at the heart of India's higher education, this book will focus on four important elements: first, the idea of 'knowledge' in Indian tradition(s); second, the trajectory of 'memory'; third, the patterns of social exclusion and their effects on 'knowledge' construction; and finally, the impact of technology on the forms of knowledge.

ONE

THE CRISIS OF KNOWLEDGE

The Colonial Indian Self-image

An ancient civilization with amazing wealth of philosophical, literary and scientific treatises and unparalleled continuity of 'the life of the mind', India nonetheless was not at its most creative when the colonial scholars started exploring Indian thought towards the end of the eighteenth century. Besides, for a variety of complicated reasons, the creative springs of ideas and imagination current in the bhashas at that time were not found to be of sufficient interest by the colonial English officers. Their focus remained almost entirely on literature and texts in Sanskrit and Persian. Given the context of political domination, even a rather casual compliment from Goethe for the imaginative power of Kalidasa's play *Shakuntalam* appeared to the Indian mind as great a victory as, a century later, the Nobel Prize in Literature for Rabindranath Tagore. During that one and a quarter century—from the founding of the Asiatic Society in the 1780s to the beginning of World War I and the struggle for India's independence—any compliment from a European scholar was generally hugely overvalued, reflecting India's complete loss of cultural self-confidence. Hence, the generous praise that Friedrich Max Müller lavished on Indian thought was received by the Brahminical classes with ecstasy. He stated in a lecture to the Indian Civil Service aspirants in London:

> If I were asked under what sky the human mind has most fully developed some of its choicest gifts, has most deeply pondered over the greatest problems of life, and has found solutions of some of them which well deserve the attention even of those who have studied Plato and Kant, I should point to India. And if I were to ask myself from what literature we who have been nurtured almost exclusively on the thoughts of Greeks and Romans, and of the Semitic race, the Jewish, may draw the corrective which is most wanted in order to make

> our inner life more perfect, more comprehensive, more universal, in fact more truly human a life... again I should point to India.

One needs to note here that Max Müller's superlative adulation of the India of his imagination was not commonly shared in scholarly circles and he was in the minority amongst his European contemporaries and peers. The overwhelming majority of European administrators, scholars and researchers of his time had internalized the idea that British rule was necessary for 'civilizing India', a divine duty fallen upon them which they had accepted as a moral burden. These views, whether negative or superlative, inevitably influenced the self-image of Indian thinkers of the time. On the one hand, there was great excitement over and acceptance of 'English education' throughout the nineteenth century; on the other hand, a dismissal of Indian forms of knowledge was common among the native literary class in India. The rapidity with which European learning was introduced in Indian colleges and universities through the second half of the nineteenth century led Mahatma Gandhi, during the 1930s, to take a rather uncharacteristic reductive stand in relation to the condition of education in India. In a discussion at Chatham House on 20 October 1931, in London, he commented:

> I say without fear of my figures being challenged successfully, that today India is more illiterate than it was fifty or a hundred years ago, and so is Burma, because the British administrators, when they came to India, instead of taking hold of things as they were, began to root them out. They scratched the soil and began to look at the root, and left the root like that, and the beautiful tree perished.

Gandhi himself had no time in his busy public life to authenticate his observation on being challenged to substantiate it. His inability to do so provided historian Dharampal the occasion to pursue the matter and produce his memorable *The Beautiful Tree*. Gandhi's narrative of colonial school education in India presented a collapse of judgement on the part of the colonial administrators leading to a complete intellectual disaster:

> The village schools were not good enough for the British administrator, so he came out with his programme. Every school must have so much paraphernalia, building, and so forth. Well, there were no such schools at all. There are statistics left by a British administrator which show that, in places where they have carried out a survey, ancient schools have gone by the board, because there was no recognition for these schools, and the schools

established after the European pattern were too expensive for the people, and therefore they could not possibly overtake the thing. I defy anybody to fulfil a programme of compulsory primary education of these masses inside of a century.

A century after the Mahatma's uncharacteristically passionate outburst, if we are to take a relatively more objective view of the colonial impact on India's knowledge traditions, two significant elements deserve attention. The first of these is that the pervasive cultural amnesia about India's intellectual failures and accomplishments seems to have hampered our ability to establish organic links between the past and the present. For the last two centuries, Indians have either entirely dismissed all that we had cultivated as 'knowledge' in theory as well as a million everyday tasks. Or, we tend to think that ancient India had all-encompassing knowledge in all domains and tend to glorify that imagined past. But unquestioning adulation or complete dismissal is no substitute for a critical perspective. The second element was the frequently noticed 'time lag' between the knowledge in the West and in India and the absence of parity between knowledge production in the global West and the global South. Countries such as Ireland, Canada and Australia too had to fight Western disapproval of knowledge coming from former colonies. But the intensity with which Indian scholars have felt this discriminating attitude has generally been more acute. It would be fair to add that the colonized African countries have had an even greater difficulty in having their forms of knowledge acknowledged as 'universal' knowledge. The African reactions too have been far more pointed. As a result a whole cultural movement called 'Negritude' sprang up in reaction in many African countries.

Ngugi Wa Thiong'o, the most eloquent of the spokespersons for Africa's selfhood, wrote in his memorable book, *Moving the Centre: The Struggle for Cultural Freedoms*:

> I am suspicious of the uses of the word (the Third World) and the concept of the universal. For very often, this has meant the West generalising its experience of history as the universal experience of the world. What is Western becomes universal and what is Third World becomes local... The Eurocentric basis of seeing the world has often meant marginalising into the periphery that which comes from the rest of the world.

The colonial disruption in India's self-perception and the uneven cultural relationship emerging out of the context of the West's intellectual domination of the colonized people continued to prevail well beyond the formal end of colonial rule. The intellectual biography of D. D. Kosambi, one of India's more original thinkers in the post-Independence decades, brings home poignantly the cultural asymmetry in the field of 'universal' sciences. Reflecting on the response to his fundamental contribution to number theory in mathematics, Kosambi observes that an Indian contribution to a theoretical field of knowledge usually met with suspicion and disregard. When Kosambi proposed that the Poisson distribution would explain the prime number theory, he had to spend several years to get a sympathetic audience among Western mathematicians. He comments in despair:

> Every competent judge who saw only this radically new basic result intuitively felt that it was correct as well as of fundamental importance. Unfortunately, the Riemann hypothesis followed as a simple consequence. Could a problem over which the world's greatest mathematicians have come to grief for over a century thus casually be solved in the jungles of India? Psychologically, it seemed much more probable that the interloper was just another 'circle-squarer'. Mathematics may be a cold, impersonal science of pure thought; the mathematician can be thoughtless, heatedly acrid,

even rabid, over what he dislikes... I had to fight for my results over three long years... There is surely a great deal to be said for the notion that the success of science is fundamentally related to the particular form of society.

In my own work, during my formative years, I have often taken a position that would be akin to Dharampal's painstaking research, showing how British colonial rule in India destroyed the traditions of education existing during the immediately preceding era. I have also commented in detail on the cultural amnesia that set in as a result of the colonial encounter. Similarly, several eminent thinkers and educationists and various reports on education have pointed out the loss of originality in pedagogic practices and knowledge production in India caused by the imposition of a language that is not one's mother tongue for the purposes of higher order cognitive transactions. However, though the colonial experience can be justifiably held responsible for India's disproportionately low contribution to 'knowledge' during the last two centuries, focusing on colonialism alone may not yield the complete story of our failure.

It is possible to counterpoise Dharampal's research with another significant work of research, one that has had equally enormous impact, but quite differently, on our self perception. That work is the text of a lecture that Babasaheb Ambedkar was to deliver at Lahore—but could not—and was published in the form of a book titled *Annihilation of Caste* in 1936. Ambedkar presents in this work a scathing analysis of the social inequalities prevailing in India for over two millennia and a passionate plea for genuine equality. Dr Ambedkar was probably the most educated of the Indian leaders of his time, with degrees from Columbia University and the London School of Economics. 'To educate' the deprived classes to create an equitable society was one of his non-negotiable articles of faith. Ambedkar's analysis opens up the 'knowledge' question in India, taking it beyond the easily available proof of the culpability of colonial domination, and takes it back to the ancient times when various theological schools inscribed discrimination as a social norm in India. My purpose is not to judge Gandhi or Ambedkar. It is common among Indian intellectuals to position Gandhi and Ambedkar as intellectual adversaries and take umbrage on behalf of one or the other. The aim of this section is not to assess either Ambedkar or Gandhi and their views on knowledge or education; the aim here is to look at the question of knowledge and its formally institutionalized means—education. There is no doubt that caste discrimination in the past and in the present, the colonial cultural domination and the continued 'knowledge imperialism' of the West have had an effect in reducing 'knowledge' in India to pauperization and 'education' in India to a savage mockery of the idea of education. To take both these givens into account should benefit any analysis of the condition of education in contemporary India. Yet, as the 650 million Indians born after 1990 look to moving forward into the twenty-first century, with education as their most desired means for that movement and 'knowledge' as the driving engine for their very survival, it may be beneficial if an analysis of 'knowledge' can be carried out from 'within', by looking at itself without unduly shifting the focus to the impact of colonialism or the legacy of caste hegemony. In doing so, I do not intend in the least to deny the primacy of these factors—caste and colonial domination—in any analysis of the condition of education in India.

Knowledge in the Marketplace

Though somewhat old-fashioned, one of several perspectives on education is that it is all about knowledge. There have been other perspectives too that held sway in different phases of human history. For early man, it was probably of prime importance for his very survival. In ancient times, after humans entered the agricultural mode of civilization, it came to be respected as a repository of collective memory. Much later, it acquired the function of training young minds, perhaps in the interest of preserving social order or simply because the collective memory had by then gained autonomy and a space outside the individual consciousness of the members of the species. During the last few centuries, education has become a scrutiny regime that a young person must imbibe in order to be socially acceptable, economically productive and be approved as politically non-volatile. Just as the objectives of education have kept changing through history, the formal arrangements for its transmission and reception too have passed through transitions from epoch to epoch.

In our time, education is once again facing the need for a complete metamorphosis. Often, the sea change so rapidly taking place in the idea of education is placed alongside the question of knowledge. Thus, French Canadian philosopher Jean-François Lyotard's analysis of the postmodern condition proposed a wide scattering and utter fragmentation of knowledge in the twenty-first century into 'knowledges' pegged not on analogy but on what he called 'paralogy'. Throughout the last quarter of the twentieth century, a large array of theory delved into the archaeology of knowledge in order to highlight the epistemic shift in human knowledge being witnessed.

Two major factors—at least those that are most

visible and the easiest to grasp, as well as those with an unusual power to hurt or to please—made their presence felt precisely at the same time as the established idea of knowledge started facing a series of epistemic shocks. One, the post-Cold War Western economies started unleashing an unprecedented disinvestment tendency in the field of education, and two, developments in the field of artificial intelligence and chip-based memory started questioning the content in established educational practices. Thus, governments that were keen on cutting public costs on education, and institutions that were keen on pruning some of the more traditional fields of knowledge from the gamut of institutional education became the order of the day. While this was happening in the West, and surely as a fallout in the countries that had accepted the idea of universal knowledge and, therefore, a 'universal idea of education', some United Nations agencies had been voicing serious alarm on the plummeting development index in the global South.

In the first decade of the twenty-first century, in countries like China and India, there appeared a mixed and fairly confused situation in the field of education. On the one hand, the number of universities multiplied as never before in history; on the other, governments actively promoted the idea of education as a kind of industry that cannot be developed without private enterprise. As a consequence, in India, if one had been talking of 130 universities at the beginning of the decade, by the end of the decade the number was in four digits. We have today several categories of universities: national universities, central universities, state universities, deemed universities, open universities, private universities and foreign universities operating through franchise arrangements, some of these as enviably large as industrial empires and others as tiny as cyber cafes. Add to these nearly 60,000 institutes of tertiary technical education. Normally, this should be a welcome development, except that the phase of this explosion of institutions has coincided with the state's accentuated withdrawal from the field. The United Progressive Alliance governments trod this path and the present Bharatiya Janata Party government is treading it too. The torrential invasion of *information and communications technology* and the drying up of state patronage provided to all fields and disciplines of knowledge have, together, created new rapids, new pitfalls, new puzzles and new unfilled spaces in the field of education in India. Here is a random and merely symptomatic snapshot of the 'news' in the field.

The country has watched on television and read in newspapers about the gruesome and blood-curdling Vyapam scam involving tens of thousands of young persons whose education was not equal to the requirement of intellectual competence expected of them. So they went out seeking relief through impersonation, bribery, cheating and simply falling prey to greed and murderous crime. If this shameful and horrifying scam took place in a short calendar space, the intellectual and moral rot atop which it stands has been around for quite a while. Saying this is not intended to be a defence of the caste system—vicious as they are— but a necessary comment on the larger scale tragedy and deception of which the young in India are hapless victims. Add to this sordid tale of mockery of knowledge the mediocrity and greed witnessed on the campus of practically every university and research institution. Add also the neglect of several key fields of knowledge and academic disciplines that makes knowledge generation hugely lopsided and heavily laden with the idea of 'knowledge for profit'. Modern education in India has not been just a public institutional system set up only or primarily by the state. It is also a cultural product for creation of which a very large number of selfless individuals have given their all. Therefore, their vision and creation cannot be seen as a government undertaking ready for disinvestment when such a move suits the economy. Unfortunately, after Independence, none of the greater visions of education suitable for sustaining the innate strengths of Indian society were organically integrated with education, particularly higher education in India. The idea of producing engineers and doctors as manpower for economic development gained ground, and all secondary school education got bogged down under its crushing pressure. English alone was seen as the language of knowledge; and the easier prospects of employment for those who had access to the English language drove the entire primary school education inexorably to the learning of English. Though there is nothing wrong with the idea of schooling through the English language per se, it is a scientifically established fact that education in one's mother tongue gives young learners a far greater ability to grasp complex abstract concepts. So, all in all, we now have millions of children who simply drop out because there is nothing in school that can retain them. Those who continue have to study in a manner such that their ability to think originally is systemically curtailed at an early age. When they cross the school age and move to higher education, the institutional rot there leaves little space for them to acquire any genuine intellectual interest, let alone research skills. The college level institution too defines 'success' in terms of 'placements for jobs' and how much the graduates can draw as their first salary. What about knowledge, thinking, questioning, reasoning, quest, research and pursuit of truth? Well, they are the marginalized beings in the arena of human resource development. The sociologist Shiv Visvanathan comments in an editorial:

> The playful power of these intellectual efforts still recharges many a new imagination. Both teachers and students inevitably know such a community of understanding cannot be created by mercenaries... Because one does not understand the ecology for exemplars, one fetishes management theories which commodotise education, turning the teacher-student relationship into one of an arid clientelism, a paisa vasool model, good for bargaining in second-hand shops but a misfit for a world of values.

If knowledge is the core of education and if education lays the very foundation of a nation, the nation needs to reflect on the plight to which these have been reduced.

Education Infrastructure

During the first half of the twentieth century, the infrastructure of higher education was beginning to be created. Since this was neither the priority of the colonial government nor one of the major popular demands, the pace at which colleges and universities came up was understandably not in keeping with the idea of creating a modern nation. In fact, most of the educational institutions created were a result of the generosity of some of the more enlightened among the princes, as in the case of the Maharaja College in Mysore and the Baroda College, or the need felt by the nationalist leaders to create motivated young persons for taking forward the freedom struggle, as in the case of the National College (present-day Jadavpur University) in Calcutta (now Kolkata), the Gujarat Vidyapith founded by Mahatma Gandhi, or the Fergusson College founded in Pune by Bal Gangadhar Tilak, Gopal Ganesh Agarkar and their colleagues. When India became a republic, the government began to build universities, colleges, national research laboratories and other research institutions. The University Grants Commission (UGC) Act came into existence in 1956 (amended in 1984 and 1985) and established the UGC as a regulatory body, with authority to oversee the quality and growth of higher education. A study by Kavita Sharma commissioned by the UGC in 2015, provides an uncritical but comprehensive picture of its contribution over the last six decades. It points out that the second half of the twentieth century saw a remarkable growth in technical and higher education—from three central universities in 1951 to eighteen in 2005; and from twenty-four to 205 state-run universities. Other institutions were also established during this period, including ninety-five accredited colleges granting degrees, eighteen officially designated Institutes of National Importance, and seven privately-funded universities, bringing the number of universities from twenty-seven in 1951 to 343 in 2005.

I mention the figures for 2005 so as to get a comparative view of the growth in India's educational infrastructure during the last ten years as against the growth in the preceding five decades. Over those five post-Independence decades, an average of six new universities were commissioned every year. The growth has been far more accentuated during the last decade and a half. According to data from the Government of India Department of Secondary and Higher Education, Ministry of Human Resource Development, during just two funding years, 2003–2004 and 2004–2005, the number of degree-granting colleges rose from 15,343 to 17,625. At the present count, in 2017, the number of universities is over 760, with 38,498 colleges, around 12,276 other stand-alone institutions of higher education. All subsequent statistics related to higher education is drawn from the website of the Census of India and the All India Survey of Higher Education website of the Government of India.

The University Grants Commission was created as a

single authority to coordinate and promote non-technical higher education in the country. Similarly, several other research councils were created for promoting research in various disciplines such as medicine, engineering, sciences and social science. The figures for the student population receiving instruction in institutes of higher education show that educational institutions increased their absorption capacity between 1986–1987 (5,982,709 students) and 2004–2005 (1,00,09,137 students) to accommodate nearly five million more students. During the same period, the number of institutions offering technical diplomas, degree and postgraduate courses moved from 962 to 38,800, a remarkably steep increase. At the present count, in 2017, there are twenty specialized law universities, eleven Sanskrit language universities, sixty-one agricultural sciences universities, thirteen state-level open universities, eleven universities exclusively for women, 3,451 business management colleges and 3,364 colleges of engineering. In 2014–2015, the total number of students enrolled for all courses was close to 34.2 million. These figures are mind-boggling and, except in the case of China, simply unprecedented in human history.

Yet, despite the large number of institutions coming so rapidly into existence, in 2014–2015, only 24.3 per cent of the young women and men out of those who should have entered colleges had been able to gain admission in them. India's share in global research stands today at a mere 4.3 per cent in medicine, 3.4 per cent in science and 1.6 per cent in social sciences. The budgetary allocations for higher education are made primarily by the Higher Education Department of the Ministry of Human Resource Development. In addition there are special purpose allocations in the nature of affirmative action from the budgets of various other ministries, such as the Ministry of Tribal Affairs and the Ministry of Social Justice and Empowerment. Additional funds are made available by various state governments, since education is included in the 'joint list' of constitutional obligations. But all of these add up to a minuscule 0.26 per cent, a little over one-fourth of one per cent of India's GDP.

Do these provisions benefit every young woman or man aspiring to seek degree level or graduate education in India? More pertinently, are these infrastructures and funding provisions adequate to meet the huge backlog of social justice needs? The answers to these questions are not heartening. For example, the disparity between educated girls and educated boys has been increasing at an alarming rate. The statistics for 2001–2002 showed that nearly five million fewer girls received higher education than boys in the same age bracket. The gap in some states was substantial, as evident from the examples of Karnataka (11 females to 48 males) and Orissa (11 females to 74 males). This was generally the story, though there were a few parts of the country in which the number of females receiving education is substantially higher than the number of males. In Pondicherry, for example, the ratio of females to males stood at 13 to 10, and in Chandigarh, 40 to 27. The situation in 2015 was not substantively any different with the female enrolment lower than male enrolment by 6 per cent at the undergraduate level, 18 per cent at the doctoral level and 42 per cent at the diploma level. The enrolment of students of both genders has increased by five million over the last fifty years, but the proportion of girls to boys has moved up from one-tenth to merely two-tenths of this newly educated class. Five years ago, there were nearly 1,160,000 fewer females than there should have been in college enrolment, for a variety of cultural, social and economic reasons. The situation reported for 2015 is only marginally better.

A similar disparity exists between students from rural areas who can avail of higher education and those in the urban areas. The picture of higher education varies from state to state, with economically poorer states having a lower percentage of students enrolled in higher education. Bihar, Madhya Pradesh, Rajasthan and Uttar Pradesh have not done as well in the area of higher education as some other smaller states, or the Union Territories such as Chandigarh. The more recently created tribal states of Chhattisgarh and Jharkhand show a far bleaker picture. The percentage of students who manage to attain graduate level (bachelor's degree) in relation to the overall population of the same age group has remained confined to a single digit. The proportion of students from disadvantaged social classes enrolling for degree programs is, predictably, much smaller. The gross enrolment of students from scheduled tribes in 2015–2016 is 13.7 per cent and of students from scheduled castes is 19.1 per cent. In other words, for every scheduled caste or scheduled tribe student who manages to enter a college institution, there are four others who have missed the opportunity. The proportion of such students to students from other classes does not conform to the ideas of affirmative action conceptualized in the Constitution of India and educational policy. At present two out of every three young persons in India get excluded from higher education. Of those who are fortunate enough to find a place in higher education, a disproportionately low minority is of students from scheduled castes and scheduled tribes. Over the last quarter of a century it has been the lot of the open universities meant for distance education to grapple with the legacies of multilayered denials in Indian society. But the challenge is vast in its scope as well as in its complexity.

When we come to the question of research in India and India's contribution to the growing fund of knowledge worldwide, the situation is disturbingly sad. A lot of our analysis related to the low performance of India where research is concerned is driven by faulty premises. For instance, it is a widespread feeling among Indian researchers that the quality of research suffers in the process of providing the marginalized access to higher education on considerations that are seen as extraneous to academic activity. One needs to carefully scrutinize this argument. It is of course true that students from villages will fare poorly if the medium of instruction is confined to English. It is similarly true that an Adivasi student who has not even handled simple electrical gadgets at home will feel completely lost if asked to work in a highly automated research laboratory. This has nothing to do with their intelligence and research ability. It is the same, in an imaginary example, if an urban student were to be asked to appear for a viva examination standing knee-deep in mud in a paddy field.

The decay and decline of the idea of a knowledge institution is worsened by frequent intimidation and brow-beating of institutions that still care to produce thought and raise challenging questions. This show of raw strength matches the show of unmasked affection for the like-minded or the kinship-blessed when it comes to offering academic positions. If these happen to be key posts, they are perceived now as unquestioningly political positions; and going by this principle, interference in the autonomy of knowledge institutions is seen as the constitutional prerogative of whichever regime is in power. It does not matter then if the institution in question is a prestigious institute of technology, university, national academy, museum, research council or a public body for research and teaching. The principle is simple: if we pay for you, you must play the tune of our choice. No matter if the tune hurts the foundations of knowledge, if it diminishes the pursuit of research and destroys the ability to raise new and meaningful questions that go into making education a quest for knowledge. It is as if knowledge no longer is the heart of education.

I am woefully aware that the snapshot presented here is more a selfie rather than a clear three-dimensional representation. As someone involved in universities and research for nearly a half century, I personally feel guilty for the state of education in India. I should also add that despite the sickening state of affairs in the field, there are innumerable individuals and numerous exceptional institutions that have shown brilliance and contributed to furthering research and advancement of knowledge. However, it is the presence of these individuals and such institutions that makes the point even more pertinent. Had there prevailed a general atmosphere of institutional autonomy and respect for new ideas and thought, these numbers could have been much larger than the numbers associated with the public examination scams. The point really is that academic excellence does not appear to be the primary goalpost for education.

I have randomly stated the grievances to suggest, in passing, that there are substantially many of them that deserve endorsement. Even a casual visit to any faculty room in any of India's universities and colleges would be enough to convince one that it is the grounds on which these 'grouses' emerge that really would be enough to offer a pathology of education and the condition of knowledge in India. Yet it would be pertinent to ask if the lack of adequate infrastructure, absence of genuine autonomy within the educational institutions, departments within those institutions and the individuals engaged in teaching and research in those departments, and a relatively poor funding provision are the only and the ultimate reasons for India's low research output and academic performance. Without denying the gravity of the hindrances to knowledge production in India, it may yet be useful to set aside these difficulties faced by the academic community and posed by it as a framework for analysis. They tell us nothing significant about how in human history knowledge came to be produced, transmitted and acquired. Therefore, I would like to have a slightly different take on these issues. My comments so far would have, I hope, made it amply clear that I am mindful of the historical, structural and institutional challenges faced by the knowledge producing community in India, and I have no intention of undermining the intensity or the importance of those factors. Over the last two centuries, thinkers of all hues have debated the nature of 'knowledge' relevant for the rapidly modernizing country. Towards the end of the eighteenth century, the debate was focused on the need to choose between Western forms of knowledge and the traditional Indian forms. Subsequently, various social reformers and thinkers attempted to bring about an eclectic synthesis of these two essentially divergent perspectives of learning. Since Independence, repeated attempts have been made to shape regulatory institutions and educational processes so as to be able to generate educated minds expected to contribute to the progress and growth of India. Yet there generally has been a pervasive dissatisfaction about education, the abilities of educational institutions and research and generation of knowledge.

TWO

MEMORY AND KNOWLEDGE

In this chapter, I would like to take up the question of what knowledge is as understood in some of the Indian philosophical schools. 'Knowledge' is a concept, like many other concepts such as 'truth', 'love' and 'freedom', that we generally take for granted. Everybody probably knows what it means; but with an equal degree of probability no one may be able to say precisely what it means. In the language of philosophy, it is one of those eternally contestable concepts. Its meaning appears to have changed from century to century and from civilization to civilization. What the ancient Babylonian and Sumerian people considered knowledge was by no means even halfway acceptable to their Greek and Roman successors. If the Greeks based all of their sciences on the firm belief that the universe was shaped like a cube, the Europeans after Johannes Kepler and Nicolaus Copernicus based all their sciences on a completely different belief that it is cyclical. In our time, 'knowledge' has more or less entirely rejected those axioms and the ideas arising out of them. The term used for describing any profoundly fundamental shift in the very basis of a given body of knowledge is 'epistemic shift'. Despite these periodic epistemic shifts affecting what constitutes knowledge, there has been a relatively steadier idea of 'knowing'. That is to say, knowledge as a verb (which grammatically it is not) is far more constant in its connotation than knowledge as a noun. In this chapter, we shall be using 'knowledge' in its verbal sense. When we move to the next section, we shall be using the term more in its sense as a noun.

The pre-colonial philosophical thought in India—beginning with the Upanishads and passing through the metaphysical and non-theological darshan-schools, Buddhist, Jain and Sufi world views and the Bhakti literature and folk traditions—is replete with interpretations of what 'knowing' involves. The Bhagavad Gita devotes three chapters to an engaged discussion on what enables us 'to know', what effects knowing has on the knower's consciousness, and how that 'affective knowing' dissolves all dualities, leading to a unity between the known and the knower, thus making any 'affective knowing' entirely redundant. 'Jnani nityayukta eka bhakti-vishishyate'. (The man of knowledge, endowed with constant steadfastness and one pointed devotion excels). The latter part of this verse postulates that the consciousness of the 'trying-to-know' knower and that of the 'all-knowing-knower' merge together. Knowledge, jnana, therefore, is the dissolution of dualities and attainment of unity.

The Kena Upanishad comments on the need for the dissolution of the consciousness 'trying-to-know': 'kenesitam patati presitam manah kena pranah prathamah pratiti yuktah.' (By who willed and directed does the mind light on its objects? By who commanded does life the first, move?) In answer to this question, it proposes, 'That which is not thought by the mind but by which, they say, the mind is thought…That which is not seen by the eye but by which the eyes are seen. That which is not heard by the ear but by which the ears are heard…that which is not breathed by life, but by which life breathes; that verily, know thou, is Brahman…' Therefore, knowing the Brahman is made the ultimate purpose of knowing of any kind, and knowing anything outside of Brahman is seen as a false knowing or non-knowing. And in the Brahman, there is no individual 'I' but only the pure cosmic self, and knowledge can only be subjective and never objective. The Kena Upanishad further asserts the perspective by posing a paradox: 'To whomever it is not known, to him it is known; to whomsoever it is known, he does not know,' which according to S. Radhakrishnan implies, '*Brahman* cannot be comprehended as an object of knowledge. He can be realized as the subject of all knowledge.' And this is precisely where the Buddha decided to take up an argument with the philosophy of the Upanishads.

As the young prince Gautama, the Buddha had felt deeply moved by old age, disease, death and poverty. He left his palace in search of a way of getting beyond these afflictions. He attended sermons in schools preaching Upanishadic philosophy, but he remained unsatisfied with the idea of salvation for oneself alone. He continued to wander, sad at heart that he had not found the way as yet. Being struck by a limitless remorse, he decided to fast and meditate on the human condition. The enlightenment realized by him formed Buddha's 'theory of knowledge'. His state is described in the Buddhist texts as vajralike samadhi—indestructible concentration—involving a movement from prajna (intense intellect), through karuna (utmost compassion) to jnana (the highest wisdom). The term jnana cannot be equated with 'knowledge'. For the Buddha, treading the path from prajna to jnana is knowledge, with both prajna and jnana, by themselves, being quite distinct from it. While the Buddha did not accept the totality of the Upanishadic Brahman denying the human agency, he did nonetheless accept the idea of knowledge as a process rather than an end product.

As his end came in sight, the Buddha spoke to his disciple Subhuti:

> I have a truth to declare unto you! If a good disciple, whether man or woman, were to bestow in the exercise of charity, an abundance of the seven treasures, sufficient to fill as many boundless universes as there would be grains of sand in these innumerable rivers, would the cumulative merit of such a disciple be considerable?
>
> Subhuti replied, 'Very considerable, Honoured of the Worlds!'
>
> The Lord Buddha then declared unto Subhuti, 'If a good disciple, whether man or woman, were with implicit faith to adhere to a stanza of this Scriptures, and diligently explain it to others, the consequent merit would be relatively greater than the other.'
>
> Upon that occasion, Subhuti enquired of the Lord Buddha, 'Honoured of the Worlds! By what name shall this Scripture be known that we may

regard it with reverence?'

The Lord Buddha replied, 'Subhuti, this Scripture shall be known as *The Diamond Sutra*, "The Transcendent Wisdom", by means of which we reach "The Other Shore". But what think you? Did the Lord Buddha formulate a precise system of law or doctrine?'

Subhuti replied, 'Honoured of the Worlds! The Lord Buddha did not.'

What he had formulated was the process of transforming *prajna* into *jnana* through a realization of compassion.

Nearly a millennium and a half after Buddha, another remarkable thinker Abhinavagupta postulated that 'the knowledge of Truth is just another name for the knowledge of the Self'. For him, all experience and all dramatic sentiments were justified in their ability to evoke the experience of that which is 'permanent nature', the 'sthayibhava' of 'moksha'. Knowledge for him was, thus, 'realizing' and not a (or the) 'realization'.

Given this emphasis on the process of 'knowing' as the primary justification for the search, whether for truth or for self, it was but natural that the pedagogies for intergenerational transmission of wisdom (what we call 'education') and the typologies of what was known or worth knowing (what we call 'disciplines') were oriented towards quickening the process of knowing rather than consolidating the object called knowledge. The formulation of taxonomies, classification of accumulated knowledge and descriptions of disciplines remain critically dependent on a civilization's understanding of memory. It would, of course, be an injustice to the genius of ancient Indian scholarship if we overlook the ability of scholars to formulate elaborate schema for every field of knowledge known to them. For instance, the aesthetic experience in drama was classified by the theorist Bharata Muni in his *Natya Shastra* into eight types, the rasas, together with the details of the constant emotions, transitory emotions and the related actions on stage. In Dhananjaya's *Natyadarsa*, composed several centuries later, there is a further sub-classification of the types of plots, types of heroes, types of actions and so on. In Anandavardhana's *Dhvanyaloka*, we get to see elaborate taxonomies of emotive states, and he expounds in detail the sub-classes of 'poetic texture' produced differently by compounds, medium-sized compounds and long compounds. Similarly, the ancient Tamil theoretical text *Tolkapiyyum*, of the same period as the *Natya Shastra*, has an amazing range of microscopic sub-classifications of every aspect of linguistic expression. For instance, it distributes diction into four types:

> Words used in poetry are *Iyarcol, Thirisol, Thisaiccol* and *Vadasol*. Of them, *Iyarcol* words are those which are used in conformity with the usage of Tamil and without change in their meanings. The *Thirisol* words are of two kinds which are synonyms and homonyms. *Thisaiccol* or the dialectical words are those which are spoken with their meanings unchanged in the twelve divisions of Tamil land where correct Tamil is in use. The words of Northern languages, *Vadasol*, become fit to be used in Tamil when they adopt the Tamil phonetics discarding their northern ones.

One could not have asked for more elaborate taxonomy of dialects and their literary use. This kind of minute classification marks all fields of knowledge in ancient and medieval India including medicine, physiology, botany, chemistry, metallurgy, linguistics, mathematics, astronomy, drama, dance and music. The fields of knowledge went through a number of modifications during medieval times, particularly after the main languages of knowledge transactions—Tamil, Pali, Sanskrit—were replaced by modern Indian languages such as modern Tamil, Malayalam, Telugu, Kannada, Marathi, Gujarati, Bangla, Oriya, Assamiya, Punjabi, Kashmiri, etc. New categories were added to the previously existing taxonomies and some of the earlier categories were dropped. This transition is most evident from the eleventh to the thirteenth century. Thus, Abhinavagupta added the shant-rasa as an aesthetic experience to the gamut proposed by Bharata a millennium before him; Mammata added more sub-types to Dhananjaya's classification of poetic arts; the poet-saints added further concepts to the previously existing range of metaphysical concepts; musicians added more ragas, gatis—musical structures and patterns; cartographers added new ways of doing cartography; arithmetic accepted a range of new weights, measures and units of counting.

This process of renewing and expanding the established disciplines was significantly quickened after paper came into use as a means for recording computations, archives, philosophical arguments and writing treatises. This is exactly how knowledge deepens in a given civilization and disciplines of knowledge evolve. It should be mentioned, however, that the schools of thought taken into account in the foregoing discussion have all been based on certain iconic texts available to us. It is these iconic texts that form the basis of the history of Indian philosophy, literature and culture. The history has remained seriously lopsided as it does not take into account the knowledge traditions of the communities that were left out of the spectrum of formal education and knowledge production. Here, the term 'formal education' is not being used to mean 'institutional education'. It is also not being used to draw a distinction between the oral traditions and the written traditions of knowledge. In India, before printing became the commonly used mode for reproduction of texts, almost all of the important texts came down to us primarily through oral recitations. Hence, in the pre-modern Indian context, the term 'formal' should be understood as having a significantly different connotation. It points to the distinction between 'oral, but sanctified or canonized' and 'oral, but non-canonized'. The non-canonized knowledge traditions belonged to the larger sections of the 'knowledge producers', mainly the indigenous communities—the Adivasis—and the communities that were disparaged as 'untouchables' and the Shudras. These communities, as they uneasily coexisted with the non-Shudras, continued to develop their own technique of dealing with natural forces and natural resources. They developed their own stories of the origin of the world and their independent cosmologies, leading to their own interpretation of the universe and concepts like 'time' and 'space'. Though the Vedas had in them seventy-two metrical forms of verse, the non-canonized communities developed their own meters. Though Bharata had organized the dramatic performance through his *Natya Shastra*, the non-canonized continued to develop their entirely different forms of theatre. Though Ayurveda had evolved a certain kind of understanding of the human body, the non-canonized evolved their own, and strikingly different, understanding of human anatomy. All such 'knowledge' was brought down through generations of the non-canonized through apprenticeship and oral transmission. But in these communities the attitude to the distinction between knowledge and labour was remarkably different from the one that prevailed among the holders of the canonized knowledge. As a result, a single and comprehensive formulation of an Indian body of 'universal knowledge' remained unattainable in pre-modern India.

Yet it is possible to argue that though sanctified memory and non-sanctified memory continued to exist and grow in largely unrelated canons, the creation of any 'universal knowledge' was not the primary objective of the pursuit of knowledge in India. This counter-argument, entirely valid as it is, would point to the centrality given to 'intuition' in acquiring knowledge. The knowledge traditions, in all canons whether tribal, agrarian, shamanic, Buddhist, Nyaya, Jaina, Sankhya or Upanishadic, all maintained that the fountainhead of knowledge is the individual consciousness. It springs from within, for it is a priori to the human consciousness, already in the being. The Bhagavad Gita states unambiguously that 'knowledge is to be seen getting realized, which the confused ones never do. It is only those who approach it with their gnanachakshu who can see it. 'Utkramantam sthitam vapi bhunjanam va gunanvitam.Vimudha-nanu pashyanti, pashyati gnanachakshu-sah.' It does not 'dawn upon' but 'emerges or springs up' as the Sphota theory of meaning most eloquently proposes. Hence, various knowledge traditions spoke of the 'gnanachakshu' (the knowledge-eye which opens through concentration). In this process, 'intuition' not 'memory' acquires primacy. Even as recently as 2014, A. P. J. Abdul Kalam, the former president of India, while writing on 'innovation' in education places in the epigraph of his book, a 2,500-year-old verse from Patanjali showing the centrality of intuition in knowledge production, 'Your mind transcends limitations, your consciousness expands in every direction, and you find yourself in a new, great and wonderful world,' and adds, 'Why don't our present and future leaders, irrespective of which party they belong to, our scientific community, our industrial leadership and our farmers and administrators, and above all our 600 million-strong youth, look every day at this wonderful message...?'

There was an exception though to India's adherence to intuition as the non-negotiable foundation of knowledge. This emerged from the Lokayata school of the materialists initiated by Charvaka. Describing the intellectual ethos of India during the closing centuries of the millennium before Christ, Wendy Doniger states:

> A number of groups engaged in friendly intellectual combat at this time. Those were probably early adherents of what were to become the six major philosophical schools of Hinduism: Critical Inquiry (*Mimansa*), Logic (*Nyaya*), Particularism (*Vesisika*), Numbers (*Sankhya*), Yoga and Vedanta. *Ajivikas* (contemporaries of Jainas and Buddhists) rejected free will, an essential component of the doctrine of *Karma*. *Lokayatas* ('This worldly' people also called Materialists and Charvakas, followers of a founder named Charvaka) not only rejected the doctrine of reincarnation…but believed that physical sense data were the only source of knowledge…

In the subsequent centuries the followers of the Lokayatas were driven out of the social fold and intellectual debates. The memory-based universal knowledge, of which civilizations seek to build an objective stock, has correspondingly objective ways of validation. But validation of intuition through no objective criteria is possible. Therefore, the measure of authenticity, the mark of validation, and the ways of recognizing 'new theory' in Indian traditions of knowledge depended primarily on approval by peers or superiors in the intuition networks. Also, it was customary in ancient and medieval times for exponents of any new theory to make special efforts to convince his audiences—students, peers or readers— that the theory being newly proposed indeed had at some earlier time been propounded by his forerunners or some preceding philosopher. The 'new' theory drew its validation from being shown as already existing in the older tradition.

India's exposure to Western forms of knowledge during the colonial era and the confrontation between the two distinct traditions of knowledge within the framework of the unequal relationship brought the 'validity' of Indian knowledge canons close to a crisis of existence. Acknowledging it, Jawaharlal Nehru records in his *Discovery of India* that while the British rulers had been far less civilized in the past as compared to the pre-colonial Indians, during the two centuries of the colonial era a new phenomenon had been arising in Europe and energizing the British. It was the phenomenon called 'modernity':

> There was more literacy in India than in England or the rest of Europe, though education was strictly traditional. Probably, there were more

civic amenities also. The general condition of the masses in Europe was very backward and deplorable and compared unfavourably with the conditions prevailing in India. But there was this vital difference: new forces and living currents were working invisibly in Western Europe, bringing change in their train; in India, conditions were far more static.

Once begun towards the close of the eighteenth century, the 'vital difference' continues to remain unbridged to our time. For an understanding of this crisis in the context of modern Indian universities it should be useful to know the nature of the interdependence between memory and knowledge and how India relates to 'universal knowledge'.

Evolution of Memory and the Formation of Disciplines

Throughout human history, man has attempted to extract methods of representation of natural phenomena by using various ingenious methods of encrypting the formal features of the phenomena. These attempts, from ancient Egyptian hieroglyphs to Greek trigonometry and medieval European magical-code languages, had essentially aimed at storing human experiences in ways that would make them 'portable', giving them life beyond their natural life. The desire to represent, store, transact and to pass on to the succeeding generations what humans 'know' culminated in the seventeenth century French thinker Gottfried Leibniz's conceptualization of a 'pure language', a language of signs that did not have any meaning at all by themselves but had the ability to represent constant and entirely non-subjective meanings (as in mathematical symbols). This was his 'logical calculi'. His attempt was preceded by a number of similar attempts made towards exploring methods of representing ideas and arriving at abstractions of abstractions. During the historical phase of transition from the use of Latin to that of the modern European languages for intellectual and imaginative expression, more particularly in the sixteenth and the seventeenth century, the obsessive attraction for inventing a symbolic method for 'stating knowledge' made it possible for European scholars to arrive at sorting ideas in terms of what came to be accepted as 'universal science'. Thus, in 1582, Giordano Bruno came up with the idea, as summarized by his commentator Paolo Rossi, that combining 'associations of ideas' in manageable symbolic strings would help to hold a vast amount of knowledge in a relatively small band of human memory:

> Through the artificial retention of the 'chains' (or relations between the 'shadows') in the mind, one can reconstruct, by means of a gradual process of purification, the connections which exist between the ideas themselves. The contemplation of the unity which is hidden in the confused plurality of appearances leads to a rational understanding of ideal relations.

A century later, in 1675, Leibniz proposed his celebrated aphorism 'existere nihil aliud esse quam harmonicum esse (to exist is nothing other than to be harmonious). In that span of a century and a half, from Bruno to Leibniz, Europe had discovered the ability of the human mind to reduce diverse perceptions to a 'harmonised understanding' capable of being stated in abstract terms. This ability is what is described in philosophical terms as 'rationality'. If René Descartes gave to Europe the philosophical basis for its rationality, often highlighted through his claim 'je pense, donc je suis' (I think, therefore I am), Bruno, Leibniz and their contemporaries gave Europe the 'method' of stabilizing knowledge on the bedrock of rationality. These historical factors would not be of any direct relevance to an analysis of the trajectory of 'knowledge' in India, or any other civilization had it not been for the fact that they clearly point to the use of memory for encrypting and classifying knowledge. The history of 'sorting out and storing ideas' in Europe is also of interest to us as, in the process, memory gets completely transmuted from being just a commonly shared heritage of human societies to a higher order platform for commanding and canonizing the cerebral acts of humans, resulting in the idea of a universal knowledge—the real business of universities.

In Indian traditions of learning, memory had been a central interest from the earliest times. In fact, what was worth learning was described by the term 'smriti' ('remembering' as well as 'the remembered'). The Bhagavad Gita contains a rather categorical pronouncement that weakening of 'smriti' leads to destruction of the intellect—smriti-branshat buddhi-nash. In ancient Indian literature and theoretical compositions, special care was taken to aid and facilitate easy remembering of the text by introducing various accessible mnemonic tools, quite akin to the Ciceronean use of memory. The larger part of ancient Indian literature, of diverse philosophical schools, was preserved through memorization with a very high standard of accuracy. There is no other civilization in the world that insisted on developing memory as the most central tool of learning with such obsessive interest as was done in India for centuries. Probably, the difference between the turn that the seventeenth century use of memory took in Europe and the use of memory in the history of ideas in India was that the idea of a 'science of knowledge', or a universal knowledge' did not find favour with those who held knowledge.

The idea of knowledge as 'knowing', bringing intellect closer to intuition, together with the sophisticated use of memory for a flawless reproduction of the texts from the past, had resulted in 'apprenticeship' becoming, as stated earlier, the most favoured mode of receiving and giving education in India. It was favoured not only for those disciplines such as medicine, chemistry, sculpture, architecture, metallurgy, dance, music and crafts, in which skills constitute the major part of understanding, but also for the disciplines in which the ability for abstraction and raising new questions form the core, such as philosophy, poetry, mathematics and astronomy. In combination with the social segregation that set in within Indian society more than 2,000 years ago, the internship mode of cultivating knowledge became a formidable hindrance to the producing of any genuinely 'universal science'. While highly accurate memorization continued to be the tool for storing developments in ideas, the access to such memorization was restricted by the social status of a person. The result was that in pre-colonial times two broad streams of memory-based knowledge spectrums continued to coexist without much of a possibility for mutual exchange and cross-fertilization: one, the spectrum of the memory traditions of those who had access to abstract symbols, including writing, and two, the spectrum of the memory traditions of those who were prevented from attempting symbolic abstractions.

In India's literary past, most of the linguistic creativity has been in the oral tradition. Though people knew how to write, writing was not used as a means of educating the next generation about these compositions. This is not to deny that we had written matter even in Harappan times, and a tremendous era of literary productivity in ancient Tamil and post-Vedic Sanskrit; but by and large, knowledge, literature and memory were handed down not through writing but through speech and oral media. What developed in India as oral tradition was not limited to 'writing' on walls, textile surfaces and in figurative ritual designs, but included compositions of texts, documents or what one describes as 'manuscripts'. They follow the logic of speech and the logic of orthography. The aim here is not in any way to establish writing as redundant but only to indicate that considering what is non-written as non-manuscript would be inadequate in accounting for India's 'knowledge' traditions.

Numerous ancient and medieval compositions have come to us without the mediation of writing, but with clues for their easy memorization embedded within them. In the pre-colonial schooling systems, the teacher set before the students a part of a word or a sentence and the remaining part was coined by the students as a complement of samasya-purti. It was a standard practice, not involving writing but with a clear evidence of document, text, style and unity. This kind of schooling changed after paper became available for use in India during the thirteenth century. However, the place of the oral was not entirely or substantially taken by the written. The two coexisted in an interdependent manner in the Indian production of knowledge. It is said that Tukaram's *Gatha* was sunk in the Indrayani River by critics who opposed his humanized theology. But it is also believed by his devotees that the *Gatha* surfaced again. But what is certain is that Tukaram *wrote*. Eknath, before Tukaram's times, had prepared an edition of Jnaneshwar's writings. Though there existed the possibility of committing compositions to scripts, the dissemination of text took place through oral means. Is Tukaram's *Gatha* then to be viewed as an oral text or a written text? Similarly, with Kabir, Mira and many other bhakti saints throughout the medieval centuries, writing and speech were not seen as exclusive or antithetical but rather as complementary practices. When paper became available, scholars used paper for writing. Previously, they had used tree bark. Manuscripts were copied meticulously by generations of students and every few hundred years they were renewed. But there were others who memorized texts and continued handing down knowledge through speech. Therefore, manuscript was both writing and speech at the same time, and this continued in Indian history for centuries. When print technology arrived in this country, it was not available to every language that had extensive literature, nor did it reach every language that had numerous speakers. It only reached some languages spoken by communities from which people could be drawn as bureaucrats, or to work in the East India Company's government colleges. Languages were chosen for printing in India not on the basis of their literary capabilities or their antiquity, but on the basis of their expediency. Thus, the traditions of knowledge that had oral as well as written presentation continued to remain cut off from those knowledge traditions that had only the oral form. Towards the beginning of the nineteenth century, when printing technology started giving new life to Indian languages, the status of knowledge in the non-printed and non-written languages diminished altogether. As a result, the split between the social sections who had easy access to letters and those who were denied that ease of access was aggravated at that precious moment of India's transition from medieval times to modernity. This is not to say that all the oral traditions of memory and knowledge in the non-printed languages ceased to exist at once. But while they continued to exist within their limited confines, the possibility of India devising a grand scheme of classifying all that was known in Indian traditions with the help of a single and unified symbolic grid tied firmly to 'all memory'—as happened a couple of centuries ago in Europe—was no longer a viable possibility.

Under the impact of the colonial understanding of 'knowledge', Indians started looking at literature in terms of a binary division of 'literature' (which is available in written form) and 'folk-literature' (which is deprived of the opportunity of being written). While Indians had been all along building houses, architecture got divided into 'vernacular' and 'architecture'. Languages, spoken as 'languages', came to be listed differently as 'languages' and 'dialect'. It is with the wound of a deeply divided 'memory field' that India has been trying to internalize the idea of a 'universal knowledge' over the last two centuries. The modernizing India of the nineteenth century had to launch upon the project of creating a society operating within a shared band of abstract signs welded to memory before it could start thinking of generating new fields of knowledge that qualified to be 'universal' sciences or disciplines.

THREE

MEMORY OF THE FORGOTTEN

If oppressive social traditions, the source and the spread of which lie in remote antiquity, have come to control and condition our lives without exception for over two millennia, there has to be a logic to their power and authority, there has to be a rationale that can be stated with clarity so that it can be refuted, modified, altered and rectified. The why, the where from, the how of varna and jati in Indian civilization need to be opened again and again like festering and mortal wounds that need to be cured and healed or surgically removed. However, despite a massive quantity of learned works in all major Indian languages as well as all major international languages—English, German, French, Chinese, Arabic and others—there is no definitive and widely accepted explanation for the why, the where from and the how of either varna or jati as social and, worse still, as legal conventions. At the opening as well as the closing of these enquiries, it is customary to point one's fingers at the *Manusmriti* or *Manu Samhita*.

Indeed when one peruses the 2,685 verses of the Manu Code, the single comprehensive statement of the statutes for social regulation in ancient India, one likes to think of the smriti as the fountainhead of the varna and jati ideas in India. They also read as the most definitive statement of gender segregation and the human desire to dominate ecology. But it is far from being clear if the *Samhita* is a single text composed either by a group of moral legislators—believed to be a tribe called Manava in the Northeastern part of India as it was then—or a single author believed to be the originator of the Vedic Aryans. It is also not clear if this Manu was the same as the ancestral patriarch of the Aryans belonging to a pre-Vedic era or the one who falls historically between Vedic times and the age of composition of the statutes known as Brahmans. The age of Manu is conceptualized differently, ranging from the most orthodox estimate of 1500 BCE to the most modest date of 200 CE. Normally, the cross-references in other texts following the rise of a given text, or the lack of such references in the texts of any previous eras should make the precise dating of a text possible. Similarly, linguistic evidence based on the evolution of meanings and etymological shifts should help one guess with fair accuracy the historical period of a text. This method does not work in the case of the *Manusmriti*. For one thing, the variety of Sanskrit in which it has come down to us through the centuries is sufficiently close to post-Vedic Sanskrit, the kind of language in which the Mahabharata has come down to us through the centuries. But, without any shade of doubt, the precepts of the *Samhita* find unmistakable echoes in the main body of the Vedas. Thus we have the Purush Sukta in the tenth Mandala of the Rig Veda. On the other hand, the ninety-seventh verse of the tenth section of the *Manusmriti* is found reproduced with very minor modification in the third Adhyaya of the Bhagavad Gita, verse 35: 'Shreyan svadharmo vigunah paradharmat svanishtuthat; svadharme nidhanam shreyam paradharmo bhayavaha (One's own duty, even when less attractive, is better than another even if it is more attractive. Death in one's own duty is preferable over finding sustenance in another's duty, for the latter is horrible.)' Therefore, it is quite difficult to settle the precise period for the emergence of the *Manu Samhita*.

While a mythological Manu is believed to have preceded the Vedic Aryans, and numerous Manus preceded him from the beginning of human time, the version of genesis which the *Manu Samhita* presents, and on the basis of which it builds its entire social cartography, is several times contradicted by the literature in later Vedic times. The Upanishads, particularly the Taittiriya drawn from the Yajur Veda, contain several versions of the genesis story describing the process of evolutionary creation, a radical variation on the divinely granted creation, and several aspects of creation dealing with the spirit, the mind, the consciousness, life and the human body. This Upanishad proceeds in its delineation of the process of creation without any trace of influence of the *Manu Samhita* version of the origin of life and society. The difficulties in deciding the precise period of *Manusmriti* need not be taken as a plea for not holding it responsible for what it says. Yet the uncertainty in dating it raises the important question as to whether the *Manusmriti* merely precipitated what existed as a social and legal practice before it and in its own time, or whether it originally proposed and propagated these practices.

As a text with a relatively more certain historical description and containing a clear statement of the basis on which ancient Indian social engineering was attempted, the Purusha Sukta of the Rig Veda is the most outstanding. It describes the Purusha, the universe, of whom are born the rig or rik and the saman—the

Vedas—and later the horses, goats, sheep and other animals. Then the gods divided Purusha. From the mouth of the divided Purusha came the Brahmin, from the arms came the Rajanya, from the thighs came the Vaishya, and from the feet came the Shudra. Such genesis myths mark the early literature, particularly literature that comes to be seen as scriptural, in every civilization. In the oral literature of tribal communities in India we come across a variety of such creation myths and stories of the rise of the human species with a certain moral responsibility to keep the universe going. Every religion is based on its unique genesis story, and every culture or nation finds it nourishing to have its own version of how or where it began in some mythical time. Some claim to have emerged from the sun; others claim their origin in the moon, yet others in some distant ocean or a mythical mountain or forest. What is astounding is that in ancient India the story of genesis was used as a basis for law governing intercommunity relations. The hierarchy of the vocationally high and the low implied in the Purush Sukta of the Rig Veda was taken to mean a prescription with legal sanction. Thus, any attempt in thought, move or gesture to change the hierarchy came to be seen as a sin against Purusha. Later, at whatever date the *Manusmriti* came into circulation, Purusha of the Rig Veda, a deity with whom Vedic lore would not have felt at ease, was replaced by Brahma.

The most critical account of the process through which the formulation articulated in the Purusha Sukta came to acquire an irreversible legal sanction is to be found in Babasaheb Ambedkar's scholarly history of the Shudras. It is important to note that his work *Who Were the Shudras?* is probably one of the most open-minded enquiries into the history of the idea of social cartography in India. His thesis is that ancient India had initially only three varnas: Brahmin, Kshatriya and Vaishya:

> The Shudras were not a *varna* but a community of the Solar race. There was a continuous feud between the Shudra kings and the Brahmins. As a result of the enmity, the Brahmins refused to perform the *Upanayana* ceremony for the Shudras. Due to the denial of the *Upanayana*, the Shudras, who were equal to Kshatriyas, became socially degraded.

This long historical process resulted in creation of the Shudras as a varna. Dr Ambedkar's book is devoted to establishing the veracity of this historical process. And he does it with the mastery of evidence and argument that only the finest jurist can. No Indian who has ever felt oppressed by the continuation of the caste tradition should miss studying Dr Ambedkar's book. Those who do not feel oppressed by the tradition will benefit by it even more as Ambedkar's book holds a clear mirror before those of us who are not aware of their complicity with race, caste and gender discrimination:

> *Upanayana* was thus made a privileged entitlement of the first three varnas and denied to the fourth one. The concept of *Upanayana* rests on the idea of the possibility of a second birth, though a metaphoric one. In the initial form of the *Upanayana*, the ritual did not involve the wearing of a Yajnopavita, the sacred thread round one's chest. That practice crept in later, in times when the post-Vedic society started reading the metaphoric as being literal. *Upanayana* was in its initial days a symbolic birth, the second birth, of a person to the life of both the mind and the body. In its original form it was a rite of initiation. Such rites exist in various civilizations in a variety of forms. The Brahminic denial of ordaining a young person with the *Yajnopavita* or the denial to perform the ritual of *Upanayana* came to mean that the possibility of a second birth was foreclosed in the case of the Shudras. This meaning subsequently was provided with justifications. The main among

these was the fact of the Shudras having committed 'sins'—though sin is not a core Hindu concept—or 'chandala karma', 'nicha-karma' or 'adham karma', heinous, lowly or impious deeds. Since the idea of a second birth was associated with the *Upanayana* ritual, the justification for the notion of adham karma was sought in an imagined 'previous birth', a notion that did not have corroboration in the main body of the Vedas. One of the abiding concerns of the *Manu Samhita* was how to avoid getting into impious deeds, by following the dos and don'ts in relation to the inter-varna relations.

All these prescriptions were heavily tilted in favour of those who could perform the Upanayana ritual, biased against those who could not and starkly severe to those who were altogether denied the possibility of Upanayana. If the Shudras were denied the entitlement to the Upanayana ritual, by a slight extension of the same logic, they were denied entitlement to all other rituals. They were thus 'ritually exiled'. If they were denied the entitlement to rituals because they were supposed to have committed some 'lowly act' in a previous life, by the more aggressive extension of that logic, they were destined to engage in all manner of work in their present life that could be described as 'impure' work such as scavenging, cleaning, skinning, tanning, etc. If they had no theoretical possibility of rebirth, they must be despised as less than human and therefore at par with other animals. Therefore they could be treated as such without any fear of the perpetrators gaining any negative spiritual merit. Given the rise of this kind of metaphysics translated into social and legal practices, there was no possibility of creating a humane society. The argument was closed in India forever.

The degrading and demeaning effect on their fellow humans must have pained many sensitive individuals throughout the history of India over the last two millennia. In every age, we see instances of such individuals trying to fight metaphysics with metaphysics, the idea of birth and rebirth with other ideas of life beyond death and salvation, the settled concepts of varna and dharma with new ideas of needs and desires. As the higher varnas found the given social arrangement to their advantage, they kept resisting reformist moves. But, within every varna, time and again internal fission became manifest and in each such instance the arguments used on both sides were analogous to the ones used initially when the Shudras were ostracized. Gautama Buddha made a powerful attempt to free the Indian mind of the metaphysic that had caused the grievous social engineering. Panini was, probably, the last major thinker of the pre-Christian era in India who tried to reverse the logic by bringing in another way of accommodating all varnas in the domain of higher knowledge by validating the importance of their speech. But his attempt came to be interpreted as being legislating rather than liberating. He commented in his *Sutrapatha* that, 'Alas, there is nothing like a low speech and high speech; it is all a matter of your social position.' During the first or the second century CE, Bharata Muni who, by virtue of being an actor, belonged to a lower social class, tried to propose his *Natya Shastra* as the fifth Veda. His treatise received acceptance, but not his community. The author of the powerful play *Mrichhakatika*, probably the most political play in the history of Indian theatre of the first millennium, was Sudraka. We know very little about his life except that he was a king himself. We do not know whether he belonged to any Shudra community or if he had adopted the name to indicate his sympathy for the victim class.

After the eighth century, Indian history witnessed the rise of many sects. The early sects arose round the figures of Shiva and Shakti. They started originating in the southern regions of India. By the eleventh century, the rise of sects had become a nationwide phenomenon. By the end of the fifteenth century many of the founders of such sects had already been accepted in public memory as avatars or divine figures. Since the idea of avatar came to occupy centre stage in the dynamics of sect emergence, Krishna and Rama—the two heroes of the two pan-Indian epics—became cult figures for many of the sects. This entire movement highlighted the possibility of 'release' for any individual, born high or low, thus negating the logic on which the varna system was based. From the eighth to the eighteenth century jati became the main principle for social segregation in India. The jatis had no clear metaphysical basis. They were more an expression of difference in terms of language, region, occupations, cultivation practices, food habits and skills. But as these differences once accepted led to a particular jati formation, the jati identity was invariably expressed in terms of the specific worship practice. If the metaphysics based on the story of genesis was the basis for varna consolidation, the perception of 'difference' leading to a metaphysical view was at the heart of the jati-formation process. In one, metaphysics was the cause, in the other it was the consequence, expressive of the desire of the non-Brahminical classes to be counted at par.

Tribes: Fragments of Knowledge

It is not surprising that when the colonial Europeans arrived in India they found the social segmentation utterly confusing. During the seventeenth century, the

Portuguese in India followed the practice of describing every community with the term 'tribe'. This practice became somewhat less favoured when the British, French and Portuguese noticed the sharp distinctions between the dominating communities and the dominated communities in India and began using the term 'caste' for the higher classes. The difficulty of the Europeans continued throughout the colonial rule in India, for they could more easily understand the linguistic, racial and organized-theological distribution of society and the economic segregation of different classes. But the vast diversity of jatis, informal and non-institutional, eluded their anthropological grasp. They could not fathom how the jati consolidation works, how within the overall framework of varnas the jatis place themselves in a defined social hierarchy, how endogamy and exogamy work in these jatis and what makes a perfectly normal looking human appear criminal in the eyes of a given community. Besides, the colonial scholars had no means of grasping the structural principles of sects which permitted multiple belief affiliations.

The British colonial officers, well meaning or otherwise, made repeated attempts at drawing up the social and linguistic cartography of India. Most of these attempts were initiated to meet the demands of consolidating the government's authority, though that was not always the case. However, given the inadequate understanding of the dialectic between religion and sect, varna and jati, language and script, these attempts more often resulted in deepening the differences without appreciating the diversity. For instance, William Sleeman, a British soldier and administrator who was appointed to detect the source of highway crime during the second quarter of the nineteenth century in Central India, came up with a list of communities that he thought were habitually criminal. His compilation of records resulted in the creation of the shocking Criminal Tribes Act (CTA) of 1871. The Act contained measures for the elimination of crime and the punitive measures to be adopted; it also included a list of communities. By 1924, it had brought nearly 190 communities under its provisions. During those five decades, some officers had come up with the observation that in India every profession is followed as hereditary. Therefore, the officers concluded, a criminal's sons were bound to be criminals. Hence the law was expanded to cover entire communities. All those communities covered by the CTA came to be seen not just by the rest of society but even by the members of the communities themselves as 'born criminals'. These communities have been 'denotified' after Independence. Their population is nearly 70 million at present. They are denied access to any land, useful education or proper healthcare. They are being hounded out of every village or city where they try to settle down. In many ways, the colonial CTAs have been reminiscent of the *Manu Samhita*. In the latter, the strange story of genesis did the damage; in the case of the former, it is the idea of citizenship that did so. The logic at work was that if one is a nomad and does not want to lead a sedentary life, he would not pay taxes and therefore he was a potential suspect as a criminal. The absurdity of the two laws is comparable.

Another mind-boggling blunder the colonial rulers made in their social cartography was the identification of those communities that had not until then developed the state apparatus for their own governance. Such communities posed a problem for the colonial rulers as it was impossible to sign any treaty of accession in the absence of a defined head or prince to represent the sovereignty of the area under question. These communities were first identified and then the areas in which they lived were brought under the British Sovereign Domain through a British Parliamentary Act. The territories thus unilaterally declared to be the British monarch's land were given over to the Forest Department for curbing any resistance. The communities of inhabitants listed earlier were brought within a single list, which later became the basis for the Schedule of Tribes in India. Over 400 different communities are now placed in the

Schedule of Tribes, ironically termed jan-jatis for they had remained outside the pale of the Indian jatis from the Vedic times till the colonial takeover.

There is a widespread misconception that the tribes of India are racially different from the castes of India. Therefore, in recent years, some stem cell research was directed towards testing the blood samples of tribals. It is necessary to recognize that all tribes in the subcontinent do not belong to one racial stock, nor are they products of a single historical period. Their origins are varied, their histories are markedly divergent. The Central Indian tribes such as the Bhils, Gonds, Santals, Mundas and the northeastern Khasis, Garos, Mizos and Nagas are not alike in any way—culturally, historically, linguistically, theologically or even economically. The diversity is amazing, but unfortunately not fully recognized as yet.

During the first quarter of the nineteenth century, R. E. Enthoven carried out an ethnographic study of the tribes and communities living in the Bombay Presidency. In his study, an impressively comprehensive exercise, he listed all shades of communities, however, without sorting them out in terms of their being nomadic, tribal, of foreign origin or the varna-based ones. Thus in a single volume he has clubbed together the Marathas, Tambats, Rajputs, Pardhis, Sansis, Siddis and Parsis. Of these, the last two have been migrant communities, one from Africa and the other from Persia. One of them happens to be a nature worshipper and the other worships in 'fire temples' where the fire is symbolic of righteousness and truth. Neither of them belongs either to the caste fold or to the tribe fold (though the list of particularly vulnerable tribes includes the Siddis). It is just that they were brought to Indian shores through certain historical circumstances and, having once landed here, they continued to live here, but on their own terms.

It is customary now in our country to speak of the scheduled castes and the scheduled tribes as if just one comma is enough to separate them, but they cannot be submerged within a single clause of the longish political statement. However, it is necessary to note that tribes is a category which is not as yet fully defined and perhaps not even partially understood in this country.

There have been other non-caste and non-tribe instances of communities too, particularly in the Northeast and the western Himalayan region. However, in the colonial social cartography, any community in India had to be either a caste or a tribe. Where large groups of communities having varied skills existed without any claim to a single caste, the colonial ethnographers posited caste categories such as Marathas and Rajputs. In the course of time, after realizing that these new caste categories were favoured by the colonial government, many smaller communities with an identity of their own, accepted these new caste identities. The Parsis and the Siddis, or the Sikhs in Punjab for that matter, being neither Hindus nor Muslims should have offered a study in comparison to examine how or why caste consolidation occurs in other social segments in India. The colonial ethnography did not have that interest. Similar treatment was meted out by colonial linguists to Indian languages. George Grierson's *Linguistic Survey of India* was carried out during the first quarter of the twentieth century. He felt somewhat confused when it came to dealing with the languages without scripts. In most instances, they were placed within the category of dialects, in some glaring cases wrongly so. But in the process of carrying out ethnographic or linguistic surveys, the colonial cultural and social cartography failed to see the rising incidence of multiple theological identities—to one's sect as well as to one's varna/caste deities—and multiple linguistic affinities to one's community language as well as to the language of the state/area. In the process, the rise of liberating and humanizing sects and the rise of Indian languages that had been moving away from Sanskrit and the scriptures contained in Sanskrit came to be seen as a little less than legitimate. A new sense of identity received sanction, in which one had to have an officially listed theological affiliation and an officially listed linguistic affiliation. The rest came to be seen as informal, oral and folk, and their potential to loosen the shackles of the varna and the caste regime remained ignored and unutilized.

Considering the historical processes of segregation and oppression of the unfortunate communities and tribes, the collective memory of these non-canonized segments of society had to be suppressed. During colonial times, the process of this suppression of memory received a greater sense of urgency. The result was the cultural amnesia which the dominant classes—particularly such classes which saw colonialism as an opportunity for gains for themselves—willingly accepted. Western forms of knowledge came to be seen in India as 'inherently superior', not on the grounds of their being logically so but just because they were of Western origin—and Indian forms of knowledge came to be suppressed. The worst sufferer in this process of internalized amnesia was the knowledge of the non-canonized. The most essential foundation of Western sciences was rationality, the ability of the human mind to grasp the universe and the phenomena constituting it. In India, the non-canonized classes were seen as incapable of 'minds' and, therefore, incapable of rationality. This denial has been at the heart of the crisis of knowledge in India. It began in ancient India and persists in our time.

Inequalities

I have so far argued that in India higher education has managed to lose touch with lifestyles and histories of exclusion of the communities and, therefore, one is not able to fully access the idiom through which life is perceived outside our campuses. I have also argued that amnesiac cultures have a difficult date with intellectual activity. The loss of language and the loss of cultural memory are probably subtler factors in denial of access to higher learning. The more easily noticeable factors need to be located in the social structures and the discriminations embedded in them. The marginalized, by the very logic of the term, are presumably smaller in number than the more dominant social groups. In India, however, the 'marginalized' far outnumber the dominant sectors of society. The 'mainstream' in Indian society is an aggregate of its margins rather than being a well-defined 'other' and adversary of those margins. Typically, among every hundred Indians, six belong to 'Denotified' or criminalized communities, eight are tribals, twenty-one can be classified as religious minorities, twenty-two form the Dalit oppressed groups, and thirty-eight persons represent the aggregate of linguistic minorities. A simple addition of these figures, however, leads to the absurd conclusion that only 5 per cent of Indians constitute the dominant 'mainstream'. The intertwining of the patterns of domination and victimization of various marginal groups by other marginal groups is typical of Indian society. Layering, not segmentation, is the principle that explains these complexities more adequately. Age-old tensions between one caste and another, between castes and tribes, between one tribe and other tribes, as well as frequent migrations of linguistic, racial or religious groups, create social sedimentations of these 'marginal layers'. Thus, a dominant social group in one part of India can easily count as marginal in another part, or a group empowered at one time can easily slide back to the status of marginality soon afterwards.

One major cause of marginalization throughout the country has been forced migration arising out of man-made or natural disasters. The refugees from Bangladesh, the riot-hit Sikhs, the people of Kashmir affected by social strife, small tribal communities in the Northeast at the receiving end of intertribal conflicts, project-affected people uprooted and forced to migrate, families of small landholding farmers vulnerable to crop failures and market fluctuations, and victims of natural disasters such as quakes, floods and cyclones have to face rather abruptly the situation of denial of access to quality education. The internal displacement due to man-made disasters, habitat uprooting caused by natural disasters and inconsistencies in patterns of livelihood and food security, all render the map of disadvantage in India infinitely complex. Feudal attitudes and repressive moral codes that result in gender discrimination cut across urban and rural areas, as well as across linguistic, religious, caste and tribal boundaries. Moreover, the social categories such as the disadvantaged castes (about 1,200), almost all of the Adivasi communities (about 650), the Denotified and Nomadic groups (about 190), whose numbers and populations are by no count small, and whose relations with one another do not fit into the definition of a homogenous 'class' add to the perplexing complexity involved in mapping denial in our country. Add to this infinitely complicated social weave the religious minority groups. Organizing a reasonably defined hierarchy of disadvantage, or creating a code for measuring lack of access, is thus a daunting task in a country saddled with legacies of fractured histories, divided society, incomparable linguistic, religious, ethnic and regional diversity, and an ever growing population that has crossed the one billion mark. The statement of this complexity does not, however, imply that we stop worrying about the marginalized sections at the present juncture of our march towards becoming a knowledge society. If we consider how badly these groups have lacked resources and opportunities, or how little they have benefited from the impressive infrastructure of higher education in the country, it will need no further convincing that these groups must be made the central focus of growth in higher education in India. I need not speak about the Denotified and Nomadic Tribes (DNTs) and Adivasis whose representation in colleges and universities has not crossed a single digit percentage corresponding to their population size. Consider also the Muslim community in India. According to the 2001 census, Muslims constituted 16.4 per cent of the population, or a total of 174 million, but their representation in various professions was dismal. In 2001, in public sector industries and public institutions there were only 4.9 per cent Muslims, in Central Administrative Services 3.2 per cent, and in the teaching profession only 6.5 per cent. These statistics belie the claim of a democratic state that provides equal access to social goods and services. The corresponding figures for Adivasis were much worse, and those for the Denotified and Nomadic communities were so pathetic that any self-respecting Indian should hang one's head in shame.

Cutting across lines of caste, tribe, religion or gender, a person born in an Indian village is likely to be deprived of a reasonably decent education—this includes nearly 60 per cent of India's population, living in 650,000 villages. The modern Indian education system has its roots in colonial history, and in colonial production systems in which Indian villages were low-priority economic entities. Leaving aside some agricultural universities, very few cater specifically to the rural population, or are in rural locations. The dramatically adverse ratio between India's rural population and the institutions of higher education relegates the entire rural population to the category of educationally disadvantaged.

During the last seventy years, the Constitution was amended a number of times in order to improve people's access to the means of empowerment. These amendments have resulted in the creation of powerful statutory bodies with semi-judicial and supervisory authority such as the National Women's Commission, National Scheduled Castes Commission, National Scheduled Tribes Commission, National Human Rights Commission and National Minorities Commission. One would have hoped that the constitutional guarantees and the protection mechanisms accomplished the goals for which they were created. It seems however that one must continue to hope.

In light of the history of exclusion in India, the challenge before us is not just how to make our education inclusive but also how to make our knowledge inclusive. Indian minds cannot be expected to produce any first-rate research if they continue to live with the paradox of considering knowledge as 'a universal science', rationality as the essence of knowledge acquisition, and at the same time continue to deny legitimacy to the memory of the non-lettered in Indian history. I am not at all proposing that Indian 'memory' or anything drawn mechanically from the past can be a substitute for universal knowledge. What I intend to point out is that any exclusionary imagination of memory will inherently fall short of conceiving a truly universal knowledge. The disparity in Indian universities will not be cured merely by providing increased educational access to the marginal classes; it can be cured only if the universities open themselves to the vast cultural memory of the unlettered and use them creatively towards harmonizing ideas with a single, and genuinely humanitarian, symbolic framework of abstractions. Education in India needs to look at the question of what is 'knowledge'—which is its main business, and what is 'memory'—which is its future, and then think out the ways of inclusion in order to be able to generate new knowledge.

Today, faced with the impending spectre of climate change and irreversible environmental depletion, the life of earth has started looking decidedly finite with the end of the species and all forms of life close in sight. Consequently, in the field of learning and sciences a major epistemic shift has been taking place. Jean-

François Lyotard, in his *A Report on Knowledge*, described this paradigm shift as 'the postmodern condition'. As mentioned in Chapter One, according to him, for us there is no possibility of a single universal knowledge, rather we have to learn to live with many 'knowledges', each of which is no longer an analogy to the 'phenomenal world' but rather a 'paralogy', 'a narrative of' our perceptions of that world.

In our country, the communities that we have so far seen as 'marginal' communities, the Adivasis and the DNTs, the coastal people and the hill people, still have with them the collective memories of coping with the environment and sustaining it. They still have with them—stored in those languages that our developmental logic is unwittingly destroying—paralogies of the universe which can be of immense help in averting the feared end in sight. Of course, if we continue to insist that they must learn what we have to teach to them, they will not fare well. But is it not likely that we try to learn from them? Is it not possible that the entire society is seen as a vast university, every community in it an open treasurer of knowledge, as if they were collectively a vast reference library, and the institution of learning a co-curator, a co-supervisor of that knowledge? It is possible that if we think along those lines, howsoever impractical that may appear to one's mind shaped within the institutional confines and disciplinary boundaries, we will perhaps manage to tune in with the emergent knowledge paradigm on our own terms. This will help us not only to get beyond the amnesia induced by colonialism in our thought, but also to provide solutions to ecological disaster that the disciplines developed over the last few centuries have posed before the world. In other words, the question of 'inclusion of the excluded' should no longer be seen as a question of 'grudgingly giving something because it is politically correct', but rather an opportunity before us for shaping new fields of knowledge, novel pedagogies and bringing value back to the oral and the written wisdom generated in India over millennia, and at the same time, a meaningful future for it. An unhesitant and unconditional social inclusion is the only path for the survival of the diverse memory traditions. Buddha's proposition that intellect makes wisdom possible only upon passing through compassion is an apt pointer for the path ahead for education in India.

FOUR

POST-MEMORY EDUCATION

The historical trajectory of knowledge in India has had, despite its numerous glorious moments of arriving at truth with far-reaching consequences, three major setbacks:

First, Indian thinkers chose to keep the collective and objective memory that I described as knowledge institution, confined strictly within an ethnic 'varna-fold'. This made Indian knowledge traditions less comprehensive than they could have been.

Second, the knowledge traditions of India decided to think of intuition as their measure for the significance of the insights gained by thinkers; but in the process producing any non-subjective 'universal knowledge' remained outside the Indian knowledge spectrum.

And, finally the colonial experience brought into the Indian self-perception an effect of 'cultural amnesia' rendering impossible any meaningful and organic relation with the past.

Higher education in India has to carry on its back the heavy burden of these three historical legacies. While its stated mission is to create modern knowledge, compatible with the larger fund of universal knowledge, it suffers from the mortal wounds of casteism and colonialism. Besides, given the difference in the genealogies of Western knowledge and indigenous knowledge, it is not able to decide if a synthesis between the two can at all be attempted and how, and has become hugely diffident in the process. All three have been the most crucial elements in the history of knowledge in India over a century now. They have been our challenges without any easy ways of redeeming the millions of young persons aspiring to make India into a knowledge society. I would like to point out that certain radical transformations unfolding before humanity as a whole indeed offer India an unprecedented opportunity of gaining freedom from past blunders. One of these transformational phenomena is the decline in the idea of knowledge as universal. The other is the decline of memory in the scheme of things human. The third is the imminent possibility of finding an objective domain for intuition in image-based non-verbal language towards which humanity is moving irreversibly. I shall discuss the grounds for these three changes in the following sections.

Memory Transmutation in Our Time

The historical juncture at which India started internalizing a pervasive cultural amnesia was also the moment in Europe's history of ideas when memory started being seen as secondary or inferior to imagination. First Immanuel Kant in Germany and then Samuel Taylor Coleridge in England postulated memory as the 'agency which plays with mere tokens of fancy' while imagination, in this view, was the 'regenerative' power of the mind. In the words of M. H. Abrams, an able commentator on this Romantic epistemology, memory performed the function of 'a mirror', imagination that of 'a lamp'. Prior to this, the seventeenth-century philosopher Thomas Hobbes had spoken of imagination as a demonic force, born of melancholia, inducing in the mind 'fancy' of 'ghosts, goblins, witches, where they exist none'. He had, in turn, derived the idea of imagination as a dangerous mental process from the ancient Greeks, particularly Plato. But the German and British Romantic poets of the nineteenth century started questioning the idea, using Plato again and Plotinus. In sharp contrast to the disapproval of imagination that their predecessors had expressed, they proposed not imagination but memory as the spiritual inferior, a game of empty tokens. They proposed imagination as an order of reality higher than the mundane and, therefore, with a superior truth value. John Keats stated unequivocally that 'whatever imagination seizes as Beauty is truth, whether it existed before or not'.

Nearly fifty years later, memory returned very powerfully as the centrepiece in the Freudian narrative of the human mind, the psyche. It was so central to Sigmund Freud's analysis of mental illnesses that had memory not been available to him, the entire edifice on which his psychoanalysis is based would have been impossible to construct. The history of ideas often witnesses the emergence of two completely antagonistic and competing thoughts or impulses, both of which keep evolving simultaneously. However, this need not be seen as an instance of Hegelian dialectics. During the nineteenth century, German philosopher Georg Hegel's theory of history, Karl Marx's theory of material dialectics and Freud's psychoanalysis made memory, in the structured and narrated form of history, their main ploy. This was too close in history to the rise of camera technology leading, half a century later, to the rise of cinema as the twentieth century's most powerful collective of image, fantasy and dream. By the end of the century, image-making devices and image-processing technology have brought to the world an alternative that appears to have started transforming human existence most fundamentally. The British Romantic poet William Wordsworth had made the quest for lost 'spots of time' his poetic mission. In his view, the 'spot' could bring time and space in a pure union. The recent discovery and use of the 'digit'—now being conveyed over unimaginably long distances through electromagnetic waves—as the vehicle of knowledge is, in an ironic way, the technological culmination of that quest. The electronic digit has started impacting the world as nothing else ever has in the human past. In a relatively short span of time, the world as humans have known it for the last half a million human years—what Kant described as the 'phenomenal world'—is close to an irrevocable convergence with the digital world. The earliest symptom of the new convergence between the physical and the digital is the near complete alienation of memory.

At present, most members of the human species have started depending on external memory chips for performing memory functions that they had been performing themselves in the preceding generations. During the earliest phases of the long process of evolution of the human species, memory had been purely the individual's prerogative. Later, the collective memory placed in the social space assumed the form of schools. Paolo Rossi's fascinating classic, *Logic and the Art of Memory: The Quest for a Universal Language*, on this theme presents a complete account of the evolution of memory. During the European Enlightenment, a new order of memory in this collective space appeared as university, museum and library, in turn, offering an 'objective' basis for the disciplines of 'universal knowledge'. In the present time, with the near complete alienation of memory from humans, that basis of 'objective knowledge' is being rapidly eroded. In its place, image is acquiring a greater power as the maker of knowledge. I shall use the term 'post-memory knowledge' for describing this new field that the human mind is engrossed in shaping. Post-memory knowledge is being 'written' through digital signs that can take meaning beyond the grammatical structures constrained by the past, present and future tenses as the memory-based knowledge was.

Language: From Memory to Image

Being enveloped in language for the several past millennia, humans have learnt to conceptualize time and space as the definitive conditions of being. The image-making ability acquired by the human brain enables it to make sense of the space surrounding us. Natural memory allows us to weave together an idea of time and then to negotiate it. Both these 'faculties', first given to us by the ability to transact meaning through symbolic icons and then transformed into a myriad externalized forms, have come to be seen as being forever there as an apparatus helping construct the peculiarly human 'worldview'. The externalized forms of imagination have been guiding both our aesthetics and our collective life. The externalized forms of memory have come to form the very foundations of what we see today as knowledge—in objective and institutionalized forms. This progression in the course of man's cultural evolution has led us to believe in certain unvarying absolutes such as matter, motion, time and space. This, in turn, makes us forget that we are a creation and creatures of natural evolution. Time as we understand it, human time, is not a natural phenomenon. It is but a convenient figment of the human imagination. Ditto for space, perhaps, for the space that the human eye sees and the space of the 'seeing sense' of millions of other species are in all probability so radically divergent that any objective measure of space is no less than pure imagination. Motion is entirely a relative idea, though I am not sure if matter too is so. If such a stark view is taken of the human perception of space and time, it follows that the human imagination that constructs our idea of space and the human memory that constructs our idea of time are both a piece of fiction. They are a kind of dream that envelops all our life, being and consciousness.

Unlike the poets, scientists of course have warned us of how wishful the human idea of the world around us has been. They tell us that it is only since we like to read all life in temporal terms, in terms of a past and a present, that we tend to think that the Big Bang is an occurrence that 'has been'. Had we humans not used language to articulate the idea—language that is spread over the past tense and the present tense—we would have spoken of the Big Bang as an ongoing, ever present phenomenon, with us as being right in the middle of it. By the way, in human time, how long back did this happen? About fourteen billion years ago. It is about 4.5 billion years ago that the system of planets that we like to call 'ours' settled down to its routine of revolutions and rotations, its gravitational pulls and pushes, balance and fairly predictable motion. It is a little less than 2.5 billion years since matter started turning into life, later developing consciousness. And it is just about a half million years ago that an animal like us became distinctly like us. This animal, the supposedly wisest and decidedly erect Homo sapien, picked up the language skill barely 70,000 years ago, creating tenses to grasp time, and measures of distance to grasp space. Most of the ideas of what the cosmos is, its genesis, progression and stability are not much older than 2,000 or 3,000 years, and the scientific propositions—which too come in human language and thought and, therefore, are conditioned by the limits of human ability to express—are probably not over a few centuries old.

Given that the human brain is constantly evolving and, in the process, has been acquiring untold powers to comprehend complex realities, it is to be expected that it forces human language/s and thought to go beyond the established logic of tense and distance, beyond memory and imagination, beyond time and space, so that a far more complex multi-frame reality can be comprehended and expressed by humans through whatever means they will in future. Michael C. Corballis, in a fascinating study of the recursive brains of humans, offers an unsettling argument—that while the brain's functioning and the structure of the human mind are recursive, the structure of language is not so:

> The unique properties of grammar, then, may have originated in the uniqueness of human mental time travel… But the structure of language itself is not a matter of mental time travel… Thus although language may have evolved, initially at least, for

the communication of episodic information, it is itself a robust system embedded in the more secure vaults of semantic and implicit memory. It has taken over large areas of our memory systems, and indeed our brains.

It is not unlikely then, as the study indicates, that when the pact between memory and the brain, or the one between language and the brain, is snapped, the brain will figure out newer ways of 'thinking'. Perhaps imagination may occupy the areas of the brain's functions that memory occupied through a larger part of human evolution.

This is of course no science fiction or mere fantasy. It is the minimum logic of the evolutionary process in which Homo sapiens have been a crucially important link. The signs of the shift are aplenty. And the shift this time is not just a matter of realigning various fields of knowledge and redrawing of disciplines. This one cannot even be fully described by the expression 'an epistemic shift' as was the one during which the fields of knowledge started following the Newtonian world view in place of the Ptolemaic or the previously held Aristotelian world view. It is not the kind of theoretical shift that involved the major, but comparatively much simpler, replacement of the Sankhya by the Nyaya school of darshana. This time round, it appears, the very basis of knowledge is getting radically transformed and refigured.

Neurologists explain the current shift in man's cognitive processes by pointing to the rapidly changing ways in which the brain stores and analyses sensory perceptions as well as information. Linguists have voiced alarm about the sinking fortunes of natural languages through which human communication has taken place over the last seven millennia. They have started noticing that the use of man-made memory chips fed into intelligent machines make heavy dents in the human ability to remember, as well as in the semantic weave of natural languages. Technologists, particularly those astride the leading glory of technology—information and communications technology—have been talking of network communities as a substitute for civilizations. All in all, there is excitement in the air, and there is alarm in the minds. This is so on all fronts of knowledge, in all aspects of social organizations and all branches of human experience. Collectively, for all nations, all ethnic and cultural groups of humans, the vision of a life well beyond our imagination has started appearing on the horizon even if it has not become fully manifest, making a mockery of all that the human brain and mind have so far held as being logical and lasting. In the new experience of the world awaiting us, human memory as we have so far used it is expected to be of little use, and imagination as we have so far exercised it is predicted to get entirely transformed. Homo sapiens, it is believed, moving out of memory, imagination and even language, are poised to enter a post-human phase of natural evolution. Man and the intelligent machine, together, are expected to develop a new image-based system of communication, a new post-human and predominantly externalized memory and a sphere of imagination where multiple frames of existence seamlessly converge and collapse together.

Knowledge in Non-Verbal Signs

Towards the end of the twentieth century a new social phenomenon started emerging on the horizon of human experience. This was related to natural languages. Though no language is 'made by nature' and all of them are shaped by humans, I am using the term 'natural language' to set it apart from the languages shaped for the thinking of machines using artificial intelligence. In the past, innumerable natural languages were shaped by human communities, were preserved for long or short durations and then were gradually discarded. Thus, the rise and the fall of a natural language were not seen in any way as 'unnatural'. However, in the last quarter of the twentieth century, the loss of natural languages started assuming alarming proportions. Terms like 'language-death', 'endangered languages' and 'threatened languages'—terms that we do not see used in any past era—started making the rounds. The frequency of the use of these terms increased during the last decade of the twentieth century. In tune with the mood of the decade, UNESCO produced an *Atlas of the World's Languages in Danger*. Though so far there are no uncontestable statistics available on the exact number of natural languages, various estimates point to the possibility of about 6,000 languages being in existence. Specialists in the area maintain that several thousand of these may disappear, prematurely, within the next few decades.

In India, as against the 1,652 'mother tongues' listed by people in the census of 1961, of which approximately 1,100 were assessed to be languages, there appear to be no more than 800 now in existence. Nearly 300 'languages' seem to have disappeared during the last fifty years. This is also the situation in Papua New Guinea, Indonesia and Nigeria, the three other countries besides India that have large language diversity. The anxiety of language loss has gripped not just the minor languages spoken by very small numbers but also languages that have millions of speakers. Even within a single given language, intergenerational transmission of language complexities seems to be affected by the quickly spreading global-scale aphasia. Over the last twenty years, a large number of excellent studies on this issue have been published by linguistic and language activists. To name just a few as a random sampling among over a hundred distinguished titles, we have *Language Death* by David Crystal; *Vanishing Voices: The Extinction of the World's Languages* by Daniel Nettle and Suzanne Romaine; *Can Threatened Languages Be Saved? Reversing Language Shift, Revisited—A 21st Century Perspective* edited by Joshua A. Fishman; *Language Endangerment and Language Maintenance: An Active Approach* edited by David and Maya Bradley; *Language Death and Language Maintenance: Theoretical, Practical and Descriptive Approaches* edited by Mark Jansen and Sijmen Tol; *Language in Danger: How Language Loss Threatens Our Future* by Andrew Dalby; *Saving Languages: An Introduction to Language Revitalization* by Lenore A. Grenoble and Lindsay J. Whaley; *When Languages Die: The Extinction of the World's Languages and the Erosion of Human Knowledge* by K. David Harrison; *Endangered Languages of Austronesia* edited by Margaret Florey; and *When Language Breaks Down: Analysing Discourse in Clinical Contexts* by Elissa D. Asp and Jessica de Villiers.

It would be worth considering whether the unprecedented scale of language disappearance has any bearing on the question of knowledge, and therefore on the nature of education, in the coming decades and centuries. At a superficial level, it is possible to argue that it is precisely those languages which are not 'languages of knowledge' that are likely to disappear first. However, the explanation has a flawed logic. In all past ages, no language has ever survived because it was a language of knowledge, nor has any language disappeared because it was not so. Probably, a more logical answer would be that in the post-memory era of knowledge, the languages constructed to comply with the memory-based sequence of the past tense, present tense and future tense for constructing any narrative about the universe are no more of use. The known phenomenon of the sudden decline of natural languages in the recent past, and in our own time, points to the possibility that in the age of post-memory knowledge our collective narratives of the universe are going to be imagined very differently. In tune with the change in the idea of the universe, there is bound to be a corresponding shift in the idea of the university. The new university will be called upon to explain not only the physical phenomena but also those which arise out of the amalgamation of the digital with the physical. It is logical to expect that the physical university, school and classroom will soon be only part physical and largely digital. Libraries and books will be less physical and more digital. Phenomena such as nations, societies, animal and plant species, planets and stars, matter and movement, will increasingly be seen as digital realities more than physical realities. And, therefore, the information, thoughts and analyses related to them will be expected to be less scientifically logical and more digital and analogical.

Education and Freedom

This new turn in the evolution of the human species has the potential to be either the nemesis of the already marginalized communities or a moment for their long overdue release and emancipation. This image of the things to come—call it a utopia, call it a dystopia— is profoundly unnerving, not because it involves fundamental challenges to the things established nor because our sense of beauty, ethics and truth will get entirely transformed, but because many communities— ethnic, linguistic, cultural—and innumerable groups on the economic fringes will have to pay the cost of the transformation by having to face misery, deprivation and extinction. Probably just as the Industrial Revolution and the associated rise of capitalism in European countries placed the traditional agrarian society at risk, giving rise to the long-drawn-out conflicts between labour and capital, this great transition facing us globally will create strife and, consequently, violence of an unprecedented order. This time too the post-human societies are likely to get divided between those with access to the digital and those without it. Already, some linguistic laboratories have started publishing lists of 'digitally dead languages', with over 98 per cent of Indian languages included in the list. Already, the communities not networked are being described as 'non-civil'. The economies of the world seem to have already resolved that the citizens without unique identities can be written off, like characters in Saadat Hasan Manto's stories, as the nowhere people. In our excitement for the utopia of the post-memory life and world, it would be tragic if we forgot to look at the struggles and the plight of those who are on the digital fringes. The decline of languages of communities whose memory tradition have remained outside the canon of knowledge seems to be a foregone conclusion. Aphasia appears to be their lot.

Lest this argument is misunderstood, I must make clear that when one speaks of digital universities, one is not promoting the idea of setting up a few thousand more institutes of computer science and information technology. The increase in the number of technical colleges, universities and stand-alone institutions in India over the span of a century (1917–2017) has been unprecedented in human history. Initially, these, particularly the colleges of mechanical engineering and civil engineering, offered the promise of developing the industrial base of India and providing the infrastructure for transport and energy. Later, the creation of the Indian Institutes of Technology (IITs) was backed by the argument in favour of developing technological capability indigenously. In recent decades, information technology (IT) institutions are being given a legal go-ahead in the hope that the non-state investment in education might turn India into a preferred IT hub. I shall not get into debating the sagacity of the logic behind these steps, hugely debatable though it is. However, I would like to mention that one of the negative results of the proliferation of the IITs and IT institutes is the emergence of the entrance test coaching classes at a place like Kota, which has been dubbed Suicide City. One often comes across news reports of student suicides at such places, and certainly no one in India is unaware of the tremendous pressure exerted on children by parents, directly when they are in the final years of high school and indirectly when they are at the initial stage of their pre-school learning, to push them into the technical-education bazaar. The ruination of their childhood and the torment faced by them is a national tragedy. The number of children who suffer in the process is in the millions. I am in no way endorsing any perpetuation of the cruelty. What I intend to propose is quite the opposite. My argument is that the present moment is also the moment to escape the tyranny of the tuition class—a unique quasi-educational institution invented in India—and the tyranny of the dehumanizing entrance test regime. It is likewise the moment for India to go beyond the social segregation and inequality in education as well as to step out of the colonial impact of amnesia and the sense of inadequacy induced by colonialism. What I am proposing is education for cheto-vistar, the expansion of one's mental horizons, for inducting children to a new kind of universal consciousness and for creating a genuinely free and equal society.

The question of education for India has been debated throughout the last two centuries, and practically every major philosopher and social reformer during this period has taken a stand on this issue. These thinkers range from Raja Rammohan Roy, Sir Syed Ahmad Khan, Ishwarchandra Vidyasagar, Rabindranath Tagore, Mahatma Jyotiba Phule, Lokmanya Tilak, Mahatma Gandhi, Sri Aurobindo, Babasaheb Ambedkar, J. Krishnamurti and Ram Manohar Lohia. Without exception, each one of them has proposed an idealistic position of one or the other shade. Education for them has been variously a means of modernization of India, social justice, gender justice and transcending the narrow confines of nationalism. Each one attempted to create a model institution for realizing his or her vision for India's education. Quite ironically, though many of these were the very leaders of the struggle for India's freedom, post-Independence India never thought it practical to accept their idealism in the field of education. The course that Indian education has taken over the last seven decades has remained dominated by pragmatism, euphemistically described as 'nation building'. Similarly, Indian society has continued to exist as a caste-bound society despite our dreams of making it an equal society. Probably the only permanent feature of education in India has been its desire to create a modern nation, endowed with modern knowledge. Yet, even if in our recent past we have opted for ignoring our idealist thinkers, there is no reason why we should not bring them into the discussion about the future of knowledge and education in India. I shall, therefore, briefly revisit some of the key ideas proposed by two of them.

Knowledge, Universe, Nation

Mahatma Gandhi, hailed in India as the father of the nation, was unequivocally against tethering education to the idea of nation. The two great institutions created by Gandhi in Ahmedabad—Sabarmati Ashram and Gujarat

Vidyapith—were more expressly 'laboratories of thought and action' working towards, not so much the nation, but freedom. Gandhi's reflections on the nature of the university as he conceptualized it show that he perhaps never would have it become just another 'educational' institution. From the moment of its inception, he had great clarity about the purpose of his venture. In his speech on the inaugural day of the Vidyapith, he stated, 'The aim behind establishing this college is not merely to "give" education.' He concluded his speech with an open prayer, 'Ishwar, make this university such a one as will bring about the kind of freedom for which we have been longing day and night; and let that freedom bring the entire world, in which Hindustan is only one location, a sense of fulfilment.' Thus Gujarat Vidyapith was ideologically located within Gandhi's profound understanding of how 'knowledge' is created and intricately linked with freedom. His insistence on freedom as the primary objective of knowledge, and his reading of the two terms as close synonyms were at the heart of the desire to establish Gujarat Vidyapith as a twin of the Sabarmati Ashram. Not surprisingly, the motto chosen for the Vidyapith was 'sa vidya ya vimukta ye (one who has knowledge alone can be free').

Colonial education in India had systematically ignored the need to reconcile the ecological, sociological and intellectual requirements of Indian society with the forms of knowledge cultivated in institutions of higher learning and quite explicitly devoted itself to produce mere 'vendors' of knowledge. Gandhi had perceived this civilizational threat as far back as in 1909 when he wrote *Hind Swaraj,* without doubt the most central to Gandhi's philosophical and social thought. In it, he had pointed out the futility of mimicking the colonial masters as a way to freedom. The Vidyapith for him was, therefore, not just an institution of learning but an institution that would produce knowledge worth learning and a place to experiment with methods of learning that would help in producing such knowledge.

Gandhi himself became the first chancellor of Gujarat Vidyapith on 18 October 1920. Within two weeks of this, Gujarat Vidyapith passed a resolution opposing untouchability. It read, 'No temple recognised by the Gujarat Vidyapith will be allowed to ban entry of the untouchables to the temple.' The main objectives of the Vidyapith which were articulated in 1928 included: truth and non-violence, dignity of labour, equality of all faiths, priority to the needs of village dwellers in all courses, and use of the mother tongue as a medium of instruction. Since the Vidyapith was seen as the 'school' for freedom fighters, students participated in the Dandi salt satyagraha in 1931. As a result, the following year, the colonial government took over the Vidyapith. This phase continued till October 1934 when the Vidyapith was returned to its own control. In 1936, when Gandhi presided over the convocation of the Vidyapith as its chancellor, there was only one student who graduated and another who received a postgraduate degree. Throughout the turbulent years of the freedom struggle, the fate of the Vidyapith remained yoked to the struggle. It was in June 1947, two months before Independence, that the Mahadev Desai Social Work College was created within the Vidyapith. A year later, in October 1948, the Bombay government recognized the degrees awarded by the Vidyapith, which till then had been 'informal'. It was in July 1963, forty-three years after it was created by Gandhi, that the newly created University Grants Commission declared Gujarat Vidyapith a 'statutory university'.

Gandhi had said in his convocation speech of 1931, referring to the participation of students in the Dandi satyagraha:

> When the history of this struggle will be written, the world will delight looking at the participation of students in the struggle and how they made it an illustrious struggle. We have lost nothing by establishing the university. What we have spent

for creating it, we have gained manifold in return.

However, in 1934, after the Vidyapith was taken over by the government, he said:

> Now let the Vidyapith move out to villages... Everybody who has even superficially understood the dictum 'One who is educated alone is free (sa vidyaya vimukta ye)' to those who have imbibed it deeply, must now move out and become mobile universities themselves.

Gandhi himself was aware that the quest for freedom, which in essence is the pursuit of truth, requires of an institution like the Vidyapith the readiness to change in response to new challenges. During the last seven decades since Gandhi's death, the Vidyapith has followed practices that may mark it outwardly as a Gandhian institution. Simplicity of lifestyle, the use of mother tongue as the medium of instruction, prayers and a combination of physical labour with intellectual work continue to be the features of campus life at the Vidyapith. There may perhaps be no other university in the world where the chancellor and the vice chancellor function while performing their humble asanas on the ground. Moreover, the Vidyapith continues to provide the poorest of the poor access to higher education. Over the last six decades, an average of 70 per cent of the graduates of the Vidyapith have been from the scheduled castes and scheduled tribes. The record, numerically, is true to Gandhi's legacy and agenda of decolonizing knowledge.

Among the great contemporaries of Gandhi, the two who had taken up teaching as their primary vocation were Sri Aurobindo and Rabindranath Tagore. Sri Aurobindo, a scholar and a revolutionary, a poet and a yogi, taught at the Baroda College, where he held the office of the vice principal for a while before moving to Calcutta to head the National College, the present-day Jadavpur University. It is another matter that his association with the National College had to be brief and he soon moved out of British India to French Pondicherry to live a life of relative seclusion. His writings contain philosophically important ideas on education; besides, several of his works are devoted in part to the question of knowledge. His unique set of qualifications—his education at Cambridge, his teaching stint in Baroda, and his profound immersion in Indian schools of knowledge made him singularly well-equipped to think about education. For Sri Aurobindo education was a means of heightening the consciousness of life and existence. This was necessary as, in his scale of the evolutionary ascent, the human species is uniquely endowed with the qualities of the mind—

intellect, imagination, intuition and vision—which, if pushed to a higher plane can enable the consciousness to internalize a far larger spectrum of reality than it is capable of at present. His brand of education is called integral education, and at its heart is the idea of an aesthetic and spiritual ascension—chitt-vistar.

Rabindranath Tagore, known all over the world as Gurudev, a well-loved teacher, gave more of his energy for setting up a unique educational institution than either Gandhi or Aurobindo did. Visva-Bharati, an institution as famous as Tagore himself was, continued for decades after Tagore's death to occupy a unique place in the imagination of every educated Indian. His philosophy of education too was far ahead of his times. Tagore held that the education process is not a matter of teaching or being taught. Rather, it is an exploration into the unknown territory of one's own emotional being. In that exploration, a magical moment suddenly arrives when education begins 'to happen to the student'. The arrival of this moment is quickened through the pursuit of the arts, activities of the imagination and making learning an aesthetically delightful experience. Indeed, if there is any single institution of learning that has produced the very best in Indian creative fields during the last century, it is Tagore's Shantiniketan. Satyajit Ray, Mahasweta Devi, Amartya Sen are only some of the world-famous persons brought up in Tagore's educational ideology. Reminiscing over his days at Shantiniketan, Sen writes:

> I am partial to seeing Tagore as an educator, having myself been educated at Shantiniketan. The school was unusual in many different ways... Academically, our school was not particularly exacting (often we did not have any examinations at all)... But there was something remarkable about the ease with which class discussion could move from Indian traditional literature to contemporary as well as classical European thought, and then to the culture of China or Japan or elsewhere. The school's celebration of variety was also in sharp contrast with the cultural conservatism and separatism that has tended to grip India from time to time.

Gandhi's idea of knowledge as freedom, Aurobindo's idea of knowledge as the search for a greater truth and Tagore's understanding of knowledge as a process of realization, though unique and substantially different from one another, had one thing in common. The shared feature is to be found not in what they advocated, but rather in what they consciously avoided to profess. All three scrupulously avoided tagging knowledge and education along with the task of nation building. Something more needs be said in this regard.

Tagore, Gandhi and Sri Aurobindo, all three, were the most respected among the leaders of India's freedom struggle. In his early years, Aurobindo had promoted the ideas of Swadeshi and the image of India as 'Bharat Mata'. Gandhi spent many years in various jails for fighting British rule; and Tagore, apart from being an inspiration for Indian writers involved in the struggle, was also the author of the national anthem. The idea of India as one nation bears deep marks of their work, thought and life. And yet, even before India gained independence, all three had moved on to the idea of existence transcending nationality. Tagore had proposed the idea of a universal man, 'visva-manav', as the modern citizen of the world. The university he founded was quite consciously named Visva-Bharati. Amartya Sen's comment cited earlier points out this important dimension of Tagore's thoughts on education. For Gandhi, the Gujarat Vidyapith was to be a crucible for shaping 'the freedom of our dreams'. Both truth and non-violence were being proposed by Gandhi not as Indian values but as universal and timeless values. In Sri Aurobindo's case, in the very last piece of writing he did in early 1950, the year of his death, he advocated structures for a harmonious federation of nations as one world without borders. For all three, therefore, their dream university was an institution that had to first free itself of the narrow confines of nation. The universe, this known universe and the other universes not known to man as yet, is the true business of a university. In that transnational university, they desired cultivation of a sensibility which is free of any shade of otherness.

Post-memory Education

No discussion of the challenges before India in the area of higher education and knowledge production can be complete without referring to Babasaheb Ambedkar. He brought to India an imagination that previously no one, except the Buddha, had. Ambedkar himself was an erudite scholar, and probably the most highly educated among Indians of the twentieth century, with degrees from the best universities in the world in three different disciplines. His message to his followers, apparently in a simple but highly loaded formulation, was 'educate, organize, agitate'. For him, education was the very essence of a modern and humanistic society.

For India to become an equal member in the community of nations in this 'knowledge century', Ambedkar's prescription of creating space for those whose memory traditions Indian knowledge systems never accepted in the past, should be India's non-negotiable priority. This cannot be achieved merely by providing reservation 'quotas' to them, which in any case is clearly their constitutional entitlement. Rather, their life experience and their dreams and aspirations must be made the substance of education. It is not enough to educate them, it is necessary to be educated about them. Several hundred Nomadic and Denotified communities wrongly branded during colonial times as criminal tribes, even a larger number of Adivasi tribes and over a thousand scheduled castes in the country need to be studied by everyone. The talent arising out of that experience alone would have the necessary bandwidth that can be called 'pan-Indian'. It will then become possible to begin decolonizing knowledge in our institutions of higher learning. Decolonization cannot be achieved merely by going for the outer forms such as the language of instruction, though language in itself is of prime importance. In our pursuit of knowing that which is worth knowing from all other knowledge traditions, we need to pay attention to the languages that have not received official protection, the ones that have remained outside the 8th Schedule of the Constitution, and without administrative units of their own. These 700 languages, several dozens of faith traditions existing in them, communities and cultures that have migrated to India over the centuries, all of these must become our knowledge-substance for refinement of the minds of the younger generations. The focus on India's great and truly amazing cultural and ethnic diversity will help rescue the Indian intellect from the restrictive idea of 'university'. The institutions that India needs to propose for itself should be 'diversity institutions' rather than 'university institutions'. Knowledge patterns emerging out of such experiments are more likely to propel with a greater ease Indian scientists and philosophers into the new world of cyberspace reality, with all its uncertainties as alternative truth and knowledge.

In post-memory education in India, we have the opportunity to heal the wounds caused in the past by the varna-divide and colonialism. If India can contribute in the next few decades the half-billion waiting for their turn to be educated as modern individuals who believe in universal equality and that knowledge must bring freedom above everything else, individuals with a genuinely global consciousness while rooted in their cultural location, India will have learnt to lead the world. Besides, to receive such education is also the right of those half-billion young persons. The Indian state must learn to accept its responsibility and spend for such education. If the total political corruption involved in a five-year cycle of elections at all levels is estimated at a modest ₹200,000 crores, and if the total University Grants Commission (UGC) budget for those five years remains a tiny fragment of that amount, which is the case at present, it is time for us to ask ourselves whether we are educating India or committing a fraud on our hard-earned freedom and democracy. India is not a country only with a past. It must also have a future.

ACKNOWLEDGEMENTS

Writing this book would not have been possible without the personal care and intellectual support I received from my wife, Surekha.

This was not a book written while working in any greatly inspiring library or academic institution. It was written in solitude and quiet that the city of Dharwad, where I have moved recently, provided in a generous measure. In that solitude, many conversations with former colleagues, students and distinguished scholars kept flashing back in my memory. It is practically impossible for me to name each one of them. Yet it would be lack of gratitude on my part if I did not acknowledge their contribution to my interest in the question of knowledge.

Soon after I accepted the idea of writing this book, my life got crowded with events not earlier foreseen.

The need to commit all my time for organizing the Dakshinayana movement of writers and thinkers brought me to a state in which writing anything at all would have been impossible. It was the constant prodding by Aienla Ozukum of Aleph that helped me in finally opening my laptop one day and typing away on the keyboard. I thank her for her patience.

NOTES AND REFERENCES

INTRODUCTION

x **India's population stood at 1.21 billion:** censusindia.gov.in/2011-prov-results/indiaatglance.html, visited on 25 January 2017.

ONE: THE CRISIS OF KNOWLEDGE

2 **if I were asked under what sky:** Friedrich Max Müller, *India: What Can It Teach Us?*, New Delhi: Rupa Publications, 2002, (First published in 1882), p.10.

4 **I say without fear of my figures being challenged**: From the Epigraph, Dharampal, *The Beautiful Tree: Indian Indigenous Education in the Eighteenth Century, Collected Writings, Vol. III 1983*, Mapusa: Other Indian Press, 2000.

4 **The village schools were not good enoughr**: *ibid*.

6 **I am suspicious of the uses of the word (the Third World):** Ngugi Wa Thiong'o, *Moving the Centre: The Struggle for Cultural Freedom,* Nairobi: James Curry, East African Educational Books, 1993.

7 **Poisson distribution:** Poisson distribution, named so after French mathematician Siméon Denis Poisson, expresses the probability of a given number of events occurring in a fixed interval of time and/or space. It is one of the commonly used terms in Number Theory.

7 **Every competent judge who saw only this:** Rama Ramaswamy, *D. D. Kosambi: Adventures into the Unknown,* Delhi: Three Essays Collective, 2016.

11 **scrutiny regime:** The author here alludes to Ivan Ilich's description of school as the place that 'stamps' young persons as useful or useless, and then the society either accepts them or rejects them.

11 **a wide scattering and utter fragmentation of knowledge:** During the 1980s, the government in Quebec commissioned Jean-François Lyotard to prepare a Report on Knowledge. His report appeared under the title 'The Postmodern Condition: A Report on Knowledge'. It was with the publication of this book that the term 'post-modern' gained currency in Western academia. Also see, Jean-François Lyotard, *The Postmodern Condition: A Report on Knowledge*, trans. Geoff Bennington and Brian Massumi, Manchester: Manchester University Press, 1984.

11 **paralogy:** Lyotard implied that Cartesian logic would no longer be able to hold together the rapidly growing body of knowledge in the times of ascendency of an over busy globally spread community of knowledge-producers. In using the term 'paralogy' he wished to indicate the decline of the centrality of 'universal sciences'. Also see, Lyotard, *The Postmodern Condition*.

15 **education in one's mother tongue:** Rama Kant Agnihotri, 'Of Multilinguality, 'A Language', the Native Speaker and Education', in Multilinguism and Multiculturalism: Perception, Practices and Policy, ed. Supriya Pattnayak, Chandrabhanu Pattnayak and Jennifer M. Bayer, New Delhi: Orient Blackswan 2016, pp. 350-358.

16 **The playful power of these intellectual efforts:** Shiv Visvanathan, 'Moral Economy of a University, *The Hindu*, 25 February 2017.

17 **second half of the twentieth century saw a remarkable growth in technical and higher education:** Kavita Sharma, *Sixty Years of the University Grants Commission*, 2013.

18 **the number of universities is over 760:** All India Survey on Higher Education (2014-2015), Government of India, Ministry of Human Resources Development Deparment of Higher Education, New Delhi, 2016, http://aishe.nic.in/aishe/viewDocument.action?documentId=206

TWO: MEMORY AND KNOWLEDGE

27 **knowledge was by no means even halfway acceptable to their Greek and Roman successors:** Arthur Koestler, *The Sleepwalkers: A History of Man's Changing Vision of the Universe*, New York: The Macmillan Company, 1959.

29 **Jnani nityayukta eka bhakti-vishishyate**: Bhagavad Gita 7.16; *The Bhagavad Gita* translated by Winthrop Sargeant, New Delhi: Aleph Book Company, 2016.

29 **that verily, know thou, is Brahman:** S. Radhakrishnan, Ibid, pp. 582–583.

29 **By who willed and directed does the mind light on its objects? By who commanded does life the first, move?**: Ibid.

30 *Brahman* **cannot be comprehended as an object of knowledge:** S. Radhakrishnan, *The Principal Upanishads*, New Delhi: Oxford University Press, 1989, p.585.

31 **I have a truth to declare unto you:** Chögyam Trungpa, *The Heart of The Budda*, Boston: Shambhala Publications, 1999, pp.17-18.

32 **the knowledge of Truth is just another name for the knowledge of the Self**: G. N. Devy, *Keywords: Truth,* (ed) Nadia Tazi, New York: Other Press, 2002, p. 66.

33 **an amazing range of microscopic sub-classifications of every aspect of linguistic expression**: Devy (ed), *Painted Words: An Anthology of Tribal Literature*, New

Delhi: Penguin Books, 2003, p.16.

38 **Your mind transcends limitations**: A. P. J. Abdul Kalam and Y. S. Rajan, *Beyond 2020: A Vision for Tomorrow's India*, New Delhi: Penguin Books, 2014.

38 **Sphota theory:** One of the major theories in Semantics in ancient India. It maintained that meaning of words does not unfold sequentially as syllables are pronounced, but rather as a sudden 'explosion' (or sphota) at the end of the last syllable of a word. G. N. Devy, *Indian Literary Criticism: Theory and Interpretation*, New Delhi: Orient Blackswan, 2002.

39 **A number of groups engaged in friendly intellectual combat**: Wendy Doniger, *The Hindus: An Alternative History*, New Delhi: Speaking Tiger, 2015, p. 185.

40 **There was more literacy in India than in England**: Jawaharlal Nehru, *Discovery of India*, Calcutta: Signet Press, 1946.

42 **'logical calculi'**: Paolo Rossi, *Logic and the Art of Memory: The Quest for a Universal Language*, London: Athlone Press, 2006, p. 185.

43 **Through the artificial retention of 'chains':** Paolo Rossi, *Logic and the Art of Memory: The Quest for a Universal Language*, 2006, pp. 84–85.

43 **existere nihil aliud esse quam harmonicum esse**: Ibid, p. 192.

47 **the dissemination of text took place through oral means**: Tukaram, *Says Tuka: Selected Poems of Tukaram*, ed. and trans. Dilip Chitre, Pune: Sontheimer Cultural Association, 1991.

THREE: MEMORY OF THE FORGOTTEN

50 Memory of the Forgotten: An earlier version of the chapter 'Memory of the Forgotten' was originally published as 'The Dawn of Caste' in Fountain Ink Magazine, 2013. http://fountainink.in/?p=4479.

55 The shudras were not a varna: B. R. Ambedkar, *Who Were the Shudras? How They Came to be the Fourth Varna in the Indo-Aryan Society*, Bombay: Thackers, 1970, p. 242.

56 *Upanayana* was thus made a privileged entitlement: Sharmila Rege, *Against the Madness of Manu: B. R. Ambedkar's Writings on Brahminical Patriarchy*, New Delhi: Navayana, 2013.

59 He commented in his Sutrapatha: Panini, Sutrapatha, Translated by Ramachandra Gopal Bhandarkar, *A Reader to Sanskrit Grammarians*, edited by J. F. Staal, New Delhi: Cambridge University Press, 1972, pp. 99-100.

66 Similar treatment was meted out by colonial linguists to Indian languages: See Grierson's Linguistic Survey of India at http://www.joao-roiz.jp/LSI/.

FOUR: POST-MEMORY EDUCATION

78 **'regenerative' power of the mind**: Samuel Taylor Coleridge, *Biographia Literaria*, 1817.

78 **'agency which plays with mere tokens of fancy'**: Samuel Taylor Coleridge, Biographia Literaria, 1817.

78 **imagination as a demonic force:** Thomas Hobbes, *The Leviathan*, 1651, Chapter VII.

79 **'whatever the imagination seizes as Beauty is truth, whether it existed before or not'**: John Keats, 'Letter to Benjamin Bailey', 22 November 1817. http://www.john-keats.com/briefe/221117.htm

84 **The unique properties of grammar:** Michael C. Corballis, *The Recursive Mind: The Origins of Human Language, Thought, and Civilization*, Princeton: Princeton University Press, 2011, p. 126.

94 **Cheto-vistar:** which means 'vistar;—expansion—of 'chitt—consciousness, is a term commonly used in Sanskrit poetics.

96 **'The aim behind establishing this college is not merely to "give" education.'**: Kothari, Vitthaldas Maganlal Kelavni vade Kranti- Svaraj-ni Pahili Pachisi (in Gujarati), Part Two, Ahmedabad: Gujarat Vidyapith, 1972.

97 **'..will be allowed to ban entry of the untouchables to the temple.'**: Ibid.

98 **When the history of this struggle will be written:** Ibid.

99 **Now let the Vidyapith move out to villages:** Ibid.
102 **I am partial to seeing Tagore as an educator:** Amartya Sen, *The Argumentative Indian,* New Delhi: Penguin Books, 2006, p. 115.

BIBLIOGRAPHY

Abrams, M. H., *The Mirror and the Lamp,* New York: Oxford University Press, 1954.

Ambedkar, B. R., *Who Were the Shudras? How They Came to be the Fourth Varna in the Indo-Aryan Society,* Bombay: Thackers, 1970 (first published in 1946).

Asp, Elissa D., and de Villiers, Jessica, *When Language Breaks Down,* New York: Cambridge University Press, 2010.

Austin, Peter, *One Thousand Languages: Living, Endangered, and Lost,* Berkeley: University of California Press, 2008.

Bradle, David and Bradley, Maya, (eds.), *Language Endangerment and Language Maintenance,* London: Routledge-Curzon, 2002.

Chappell, Tim, (ed.), *The Plato Reader,* Edinburgh: Edinburgh University Press, 1996.

Coleridge, Samuel Taylor, *Biographia Literaria,* 1817.

Corballis, Michael, *The Recursive Mind: The Origins of Human*

Language, Thought, and Civilization, Princeton: Princeton University Press, 2011.

Chitre, Dilip, (ed. and trans.), *Says Tuka: Selected Poems of Tukaram,* Pune: Sontheimer Cultural Association, 1991.

Cru, Josep, ed., *The Management of Linguistic Diversity and Peace Processes,* Barcelona: UNESCOCAT, 2010.

Crystal, David, *Language Death,* Cambridge: Cambridge University Press, 2000.

Dalby, Andrew, *Language in Danger,* New York: Columbia University Press, 2003.

Deshpande, C. R., *Transmission in the Mahabharata Tradition: Vyasa and Vyasids,* Simla: Indian Institute of Advanced Studies, 1978.

Devy, G. N., *Of Many Heroes: An Indian Essay in Literary Historiography,* Hyderabad: Orient Longman, 1998.

———ed., *Painted Words: An Anthology of Tribal Literature,* New Delhi: Penguin Books, 2003.

———ed., *Indian Literary Criticism: Theory and Interpretation,* New Delhi: Orient Blackswan, 2003.

———, 'Truth: India', in *Keywords: Truth,* edited by Nadia Tazi, New York: Other Press, 2004.

———'Development', *A Nomad Called Thief: Reflections on Adivasi Silence,* New Delhi: Orient Blackswan, 2006.

———*Aadivaasi Jaane Chhe* (in Gujarati), Baroda: Bhasha Research and Publication Centre, 2006.

———'India: Layered Inequalities', *Origins, Journeys and*

Returns: Social Justice in International Higher Education, Toby Alice Volkman, (ed.), New York: Social Science Research Council, 2009.

———— *The G. N. Devy Reader: After Amnesia* (1992), *Of Many Heroes* (1997), *The Being of Bhasha, Countering Violence* (2009), New Delhi: Orient Blackswan, 2009.

Dharampal, *The Beautiful Tree: Indigenous Education in the Eighteenth Century, Collected Writings, Vol. III,* Mapusa: Other Indian Press, 2000.

Doniger, Wendy, *The Hindus: An Alternative History*, New Delhi: The Speaking Tiger Edition, 2015.

Eisenstadt, S. N., Kahane, R., and Shulam, D., eds., *Orthodoxy, Heterodoxy and Dissent in India*, Berlin and New York: Mouton, 1984.

Enthoven, R. E., *The Tribes and Castes of Bombay*, Three Volumes, Bombay: The Government Printing Press, 1920-1922.

Fishman, Joshua A., (ed.), *Can Threatened Languages Be Saved?* Clivedon and Sydney: Multilingual Matters, 2001.

Florey, Margaret, (ed.), *Endangered Languages of Australia*, New York: Oxford University Press, 2010.

Gillespie, Tarleton, *Wired Shut: Copyright and the Shape of Digital Culture,* Cambridge, Massachusetts: The MIT Press, 2007.

Grenoble, Lenore A. and Whaley, Lindsay J., *Saving Languages,* Cambridge: Cambridge University Press, 2006.

Grierson, George Abraham, *1928-2004 Linguistic Survey of India*, 11 vols, 19 parts, New Delhi: Mittal/Low Price Publication, 2005.

Harrison, K. David, *When Languages Die,* New York: Oxford University Press, 2007.

Hobbes, Thomas, *The Leviathan,* 1651.

Jiarazbhoy, N. A. 'Music', Basham, A. L., (ed.), *A Cultural History of India,* Oxford: Oxford University Press, 1975.

Kalam, A. P. J. Abdul and Rajan,Y. S., *Beyond 2020: A Vision for Tomorrow's India*, New Delhi: Penguin Books, 2014.

Kothari, Vitthaldas Maganlal, *Kelavni vade Kranti-Svaraj-ni Pahili Pachisi* (in Gujarati), Part Two, Ahmedabad: Gujarat Vidyapith, 1973.

Lacan, Jacques, *Ecrits: A Selection,* trans. Alan Sheridan, New York: W. W. Norton, 1977.

Lyotard, Jean-François, *The Postmodern Condition: A Report on Knowledge*, trans. Geoff Bennington and Brian Massumi, Manchester: Manchester University Press, 1984.

Max Müller, Friedrich, *India: What Can It Teach Us*? New York: Funk and Wagnalls, 1882.

Masson J. L., and Patwardhan, M. V., *Santarasa and Abhinava's Philosophy,* Pune: The Oriental Institute, 1969.

Mayhew, Arthur, *The Education of India: A Survey of British Education Policy in India, 1835-1920, and Its Bearing on National Life and Problems in India Today*, London: Faber and Gwyer, 1926.

Merleau-Ponty, Maurice, *Phenomenology of Perception,* trans. Donald A. Landes, New York: Routledge, 2012.

Mosley, Christopher, *The Atlas of the World Languages in Danger,* UNESCO, 2010.

Nurullah, Syed, and Naik, J. P., *History of Education in India during the British Period,* Bombay: Popular, 1951.

Nehru, Jawaharlal, *The Discovery of India,* Delhi: Penguin Books, 2010 (Calcutta: Signet Press, 1946).

Nettle, Daniel and Romaine, Suzanne, *Vanishing Voices,* Oxford: Oxford University Press, 2000.

Ngugi Wa Thiong'o, *Moving the Centre: The Struggle for Cultural Freedom,* London, 1993; Nairobi: James Curry, East African Educational Books.

Nigam, R. C., *Language Handbook on Mother Tongues in Census, Census of India 1971,* No. 10, New Delhi: Census Centenary Monographs, 1972.

Plato, *The Republic*, trans. Allen Bloom, London: HarperCollins, 1968.

Radhakrishnan, S., *The Principal Upanishads,* Delhi: Oxford University Press, 1953, Indian edition, 1989.

Ramanujan, A. K., 'Annayya's Anthropology', *From Cauvery to Godavary: Modern Kannada Short Stories*, Ramchandra Sharma (ed.), trans. from Kannada by Narayan Hegde, New Delhi: Penguin Books, 1992.

Ramaswamy, Ram, *D. D. Kosambi: Adventures into the Unknown,* New Delhi: Three Essays Collective, 2016.

Rege, Sharmila, *Against the Madness of Manu: B. R. Ambedkar's Writings on Brahminical Patriarchy,* New Delhi: Navayana, 2013.

Rossi, Paolo, *Logic and the Art of Memory: the Quest for a Universal Language,* London: Athlone Press, 2006.

Sen, Amartya, *The Argumentative Indian,* New Delhi: Penguin, 2006.

Sengupta, Kamalini, ed., *Endangered Languages in India,* New Delhi: INTACH, 2010.

Sharma, Kavita, *Sixty Years of the University Grants Commission,* New Delhi: UGC, 2013.

Thorat, Sukhdev, 'Higher Education in India Emerging Issues Related to Access Inclusiveness and Quality', 1-26, *Higher Education in India: Issues Related to Expansion, Inclusiveness, Quality and Finance,* UGC Report, New Delhi: University Grants Commission, 2008.

Trungpa, Chögyam, *The Heart of The Budda,* Boston: Shambhala Publications, 1999.

Wurn, Stephen, *Atlas of the World's Languages in Danger,* UNESCO, 2005.

INDEX

Abhinavagupta, 32, 35
Abrams, M. H., 78
Adivasis, 36, 71, 74
aesthetic experience in drama, 33
Africa's selfhood, 6
Agarkar, Gopal Ganesh, 17
'all-knowing-knower,' 29
Ambedkar, Babasaheb, 9, 94, 104
  Who Were the Shudras?, 55
  Annihilation of Caste, 9
apprenticeship, 45
artificial intelligence, 12
Atlas of the World's Languages in Danger, 88
Aurobindo, Sri, 94, 103
avatar, idea of, 59–60

Baroda College, 17, 100

Bhagavad Gita, 28–29, 38, 44, 52
Bhakti literature and folk traditions, 28
Big Bang, 83
Brahman, 29–30, 31
Brahmin, 54
Brahminical classes, 2
British Parliamentary Act, 63
Bruno, Giordano, 42
Buddha, Lord, 30, 31–32, 58, 75, 104

Central Indian tribes, 64
chip-based memory, 12
civilizing India, 3
collective memory, 11
colonial education in India, 96–97
colonial Europeans in India,

60–61
Copernicus, Nicolaus, 28
Corballis, Michael C., 84
Criminal Tribes Act (CTA) of 1871, 62–63

decolonizing knowledge, 105
Denotified and Nomadic Tribes (DNTs), 70–71, 105
Descartes, René, 43
Devi, Mahasweta, 101
Dharampal, *8*
The Beautiful Tree, 4
Dhvanyaloka (Anandavardhana), 33
The Discovery of India (Jawaharlal Nehru), 40
Doniger, Wendy, 39

education
  budgetary allocations for higher, 20
  disparity between educated girls and educated boys, 20–21
  evolution of, 11–12
  female, 20–21
  freedom and, 91–95, 92–95
  Gandhi's idea of, 95–100
  growth in technical and higher, 17–18
  higher, 15, 16, 17–19, 20–21, 22, 23, 68, 71, 72, 77
  idea of nation, 95
  inequalities in, 72–75
  infrastructure of higher, 16–26
  institutional, 12–13, 92–93
  rural *vs* urban, 21–22
  Sri Aurobindo's idea of, 100–101
  student enrolment, 20–21
  Tagore's idea of, 101–102
  of tribe students, 21–22
educational institutions, 17–19, 92–93
education in India, 3–4, 13, 15, 17–26
  institutional education, 12–13, 36, 92–93
Egyptian hieroglyphs, 41
English education, 3
English language, 15
Enthoven, R. E., 64
European learning, 3
exclusion of the communities in India, 68–74

Fergusson College, 17
formal education, 36

Freud, Sigmund, 79

Gandhi, Mahatma, 3–4, 9, 94, 95–100, 103
   colonial school education in India, 4–5
George Grierson's *Linguistic Survey of India*, 66
Gujarat Vidyapith, 17, 95–100, 103

harmonised understanding, 43
Hegel, Georg, 79
higher education, 15, 16, 17–19, 20–21, 22, 23, 68, 71, 72, 77
Hind Swaraj, 97
Homo sapiens, 84–85, 87
human history, phases of, 10–11

image-processing technology, 80
Indian Institutes of Technology (IITs), 93
Indian thoughts, 1–2
institutional education, 12–13, 36, 92–93
integral education, 101
intuition, 38–39
Iyarcol, 34

Kalam, A. P. J. Abdul, 38
Keats, John, 79
Kena Upanishad, 29–30
Kepler, Johannes, 28
Khan, Sir Syed Ahmad, 94
'knowing,' process of, 32
knowledge, 10–16
   ancient concept, 27–28
   Aurobindo's idea of, 102–103
   in Bhagavad Gita, 28–29, 38, 44
   in Buddhist texts, 30–31
   canonized and non-canonized, 36–37
   distinction between labour and, 37
   epistemic shift of, 28
   Gandhi's idea of, 102–103
   impact of the colonial understanding of, 49
   Indian traditions, 43–44, 67, 76, 77
   intuition as the non-negotiable foundation, 38–39
   in Kena Upanishad, 29–30
   as 'knowing,' 45
   memory-based universal, 39
   method for stating, 42
   method of stabilizing, 43

in non-verbal signs, 87–91
oral traditions and the
   written traditions of, 36,
   46–48
pedagogic practices and, 8
post-memory, 104–107
pre-colonial philosophical
   thought, 28
production, 5–6, 14, 25,
   35–36, 73
for profit, 14
Tagore's idea of, 102–103
through speech, 48
transactions, 34
'validity' of Indian, 40
Western forms *vs* Indian
   forms, 26, 40
'knowledge century,' 104
knowledge institutions
   autonomy of, 24
   decay and decline of, 23–24
Kosambi, D. D., 7
Krishnamurti, J., 94

languages, 49, 50, 81–87
   endangered, 88
   mother tongues, 88
   natural language, 86, 87,
      88, 90
Leibniz, Gottfried, 42–43
life of the mind, 1

literary productivity in India,
   ancient and medieval
   compositions, 46–47
literature, 49
Logic and the Art of Memory:
   The Quest for a Universal
   Language, 81
Lohia, Ram Manohar, 94
Lyotard, Jean-François, 11
   A Report on Knowledge, 74

Mahadev Desai Social Work
   College, 98
Maharaja College, Mysore, 17
Manu Code, 50
Manu Samhita, 50, 52–53,
   53, 57, 63
Manusmriti, 50, 52, 53,
   54–55
Marathas, 65
marginalization of community.
   See exclusion of the
   communities in India
Marx, Karl, 79
memory, evolution of, 41–49,
   78–81
   externalized forms, 82
memory-based knowledge
   spectrums, 45–46
memory-based universal
   knowledge, 39

modern Indian education system, 71–72
modern Indian universities, 41
modernity, 40–41
mother tongues, 88
Moving the Centre: The Struggle for Cultural Freedoms, 6
Mrichhakatika, 59
Müller, Friedrich Max, 2–3

National College (present-day Jadavpur University), 17, 100
National Human Rights Commission, 72
National Minorities Commission, 72
National Scheduled Castes Commission, 72
National Scheduled Tribes Commission, 72
National Women's Commission, 72
natural language, 86, 87, 88, 90
Natyadarsa (Dhananjaya), 33
Natya Shastra (Bharata Muni), 33, 36, 59
Negritude, 6
new theory, 39–40

non-canonized segments of society, 67
non-caste and non-tribe instances of communities, 65
non-sanctified memory, 37

oral literature of tribal communities, 54

Panini, 58
paralogy, 11
Parsis, 65–66
Patanjali, 38
philosophical schools of Hinduism, 39
Phule, Mahatma Jyotiba, 94
Plato, 78–79
Poisson distribution, 7
post-memory education in India, 106
post-memory knowledge, 81, 90
pre-colonial schooling systems, 47
pure language, 42
Purusha, 54

Radhakrishnan, S., 30
Rajanya, 54
Ray, Satyajit, 101

reservation 'quotas,' 105
Riemann hypothesis, 7
Rig Veda, 52, 53
    Purush Sukta of, 54–55
Rossi, Paolo, 42
Roy, Raja Rammohan, 94

sanctified memory, 37
Sanskrit, 34, 46, 52, 66
Schedule of Tribes in India, 63–64
Sen, Amartya, 102, 103
Shakuntalam, 2
Shantiniketan, 101, 102
Shiva and Shakti, 59
Shudra, 54
Shudras, 55–56, 59
Siddis, 66
'sorting out and storing ideas,' 44
Sphota theory of meaning, 38
Subhuti, 31–32
Suicide City, 93
Sutrapatha, 59

Tagore, Rabindranath, 2, 94, 101, 103
Thiong'o, Ngugi Wa, 6
Thirisol, 34
Thisaiccol, 34
Tilak, Bal Gangadhar, 17, 94

Tolkapiyyum, 33
'trying-to-know' knower, 29
Tukaram's *Gatha,* 47

universal knowledge, 6, 12, 44, 45, 49, 74, 77, 105–106
universal science, 42
universities, 12–13
University Grants Commission, 18–19, 106–107
University Grants Commission (UGC) Act, 17
Upanayana ritual, 55–57

Vadasol, 34
Vaishya, 54
varna and jati ideas in India, 50–51, 59–60, 61–62
    Dr Ambedkar's ideas, 55–57
    Purush Sukta of Rig Veda, 54–55
    Vedic times, 64
Vedas, 51–52
Vedic Aryans, 52–53
Vidyasagar, Ishwarchand, 94
Visva-Bharati, 101, 103
visva-manav, 103
Visvanathan, Shiv, 16

Wordsworth, William, 80

Made in the USA
Monee, IL
28 April 2026